Guided Reading Strategies

· ·

THE **HOLT**
AMERICAN
NATION

HOLT, RINEHART AND WINSTON
A Harcourt Education Company

Austin · New York · Orlando · Atlanta · San Francisco · Boston · Dallas · Toronto · London

Cover: Christie's Images
Title Page: © CORBIS/Bill Ross

Printed in the United States of America

ISBN 0-03-065332-0

1 2 3 4 5 6 7 8 9 082 04 03 02 01

Guided Reading Strategies

The World by 1500

GUIDED READING STRATEGIES 1.1

■ **READING THE SECTION** As you read the section, match each of the following peoples with the correct information by writing the correct letter in the space provided.

_____ **1.** Paleo-Indians

_____ **2.** the Olmec

_____ **3.** the Maya

_____ **4.** the Toltec

_____ **5.** the Aztec

_____ **6.** the Inca

_____ **7.** the Anasazi

_____ **8.** the Adena and Hopewell

a. built rock and adobe dwellings, many of them in the sides of cliffs

b. developed the first complete writing system in early America

c. Mound Builders

d. built Tula, a great city-state; their empire became the center of a large trading network

e. the first Americans

f. viewed warfare as a sacred duty

g. the largest empire in the Americas in the mid-1400s

h. the first great Mesoamerican culture; originators of the earliest ball court in Mesoamerica

■ **POST-READING QUICK CHECK** After you have finished reading the section, in the space provided, list three results of the Agricultural Revolution.

1. _____

2. _____

3. _____

CHAPTER 1 — The World by 1500

GUIDED READING STRATEGIES 1.2

■ **READING THE SECTION** As you read the section, circle the boldface word or phrase that best completes each statement below.

1. A **republic/kingdom** is a system of government run by elected officials.

2. Ghana's most powerful leader in about 1065 was **Qur'an/Tenkaminen**.

3. Made in China, *Kublai Khan/Diamond Sutra* was the world's first-known printed book.

4. The Islamic faith was created when **Muhammad/Mansa Musa** experienced a vision in 610.

5. **Swahili/Mogadishu** was spoken on Africa's eastern coast.

6. Mansa Musa undertook a **hajj/raja**, or a sacred pilgrimage, to Mecca.

7. The city of **Timbuktu/Aksum** was home to three universities and 180 Islamic schools.

8. Leif Eriksson was a Viking leader who established the first European settlement in **North America/South America**.

■ **POST-READING QUICK CHECK** After you have finished reading the section, in the space provided, list three effects that trade had on the early world trading kingdoms.

1. _____

2. _____

3. _____

CHAPTER 1

The World by 1500

GUIDED READING STRATEGIES 1.3

■■ READING THE SECTION Review the list of events before reading the section. Then as you read the section, number the following events in the order in which they occurred.

_____ **1.** The invention of more productive farm equipment enabled fewer laborers to produce more food.

_____ **2.** Isabella and Ferdinand united Castile and Aragon.

_____ **3.** The Crusades began.

_____ **4.** Charlemagne established the nobility system in Europe.

_____ **5.** Johannes Gutenberg, a German printer, invented a printing press that used movable type.

_____ **6.** The bourgeoisie, or urban middle class, was formed.

_____ **7.** Magna Carta was written.

_____ **8.** Spain was unified.

■■ POST-READING QUICK CHECK After you have finished reading the section, in the space provided, identify three factors that contributed to the decline of feudalism and explain the effect of each one.

1. Factor: _____ Effect: _____

_____

2. Factor: _____ Effect: _____

_____

3. Factor: _____ Effect: _____

_____

Name ______________________ Class ____________ Date ____________

CHAPTER 1

The World by 1500

GUIDED READING STRATEGIES 1.4

READING THE SECTION **As you read the section, complete the following chart. List three positive effects and two negative effects that Asian trading practices directly or indirectly had on Europe and Africa.**

Asian Trading Practices

Positive Effects	Negative Effects
1. ______________________	1. ______________________
2. ______________________	2. ______________________
3. ______________________	

POST-READING QUICK CHECK **After you have finished reading the section, in the space provided, list the three people you consider to be the most important to the events described in Section 4 and explain their significance.**

1. Person: ______________________ Significance: ______________________

____

2. Person: ______________________ Significance: ______________________

____

3. Person: ______________________ Significance: ______________________

____

CHAPTER
2

Empires of the Americas

GUIDED READING STRATEGIES 2.1

■ **READING THE SECTION** Review the list of events before reading the section. Then as you read the section, number the following events in the order in which they occurred.

_____ **1.** Ferdinand and Isabella of Spain agreed to fund Columbus's journey.

_____ **2.** The Spanish began importing African slaves.

_____ **3.** Columbus encountered the Taino, farmers and fishers who lived in small settlements.

_____ **4.** Columbus ordered the construction of a new settlement called Isabela, then spent the next three years sailing the Caribbean searching for gold.

_____ **5.** Columbus established the first Spanish colony on Hispaniola, naming the colony La Navidad.

_____ **6.** Columbus moved from Genoa, Italy, to Lisbon, Portugal, where he studied sea travel.

_____ **7.** Isabella and Ferdinand made Columbus viceroy and governor of the islands he discovered.

_____ **8.** Columbus asked John II of Portugal to give him ships for an exploration west.

_____ **9.** Bartolomé de Las Casas began to publicly question the system of *encomienda*.

■ **POST-READING QUICK CHECK** After you have finished reading the section, in the space provided, list three ways Columbus and the colonists he brought over affected Native Americans.

1. _____

2. _____

3. _____

CHAPTER 2 Empires of the Americas

GUIDED READING STRATEGIES 2.2

■■ **READING THE SECTION** As you read this section, examine each of the pairs of statements below. Circle the letter of the statement in each pair that is true.

1. **a.** Hernán Cortés conquered the Inca.
   b. Hernán Cortés conquered the Aztec.

2. **a.** Pánfilo de Narváez successfully colonized North America's coastline along the Gulf of Mexico.
   b. Pánfilo de Narváez failed to colonize North America's coastline along the Gulf of Mexico.

3. **a.** The first explorer's ship to circumnavigate the world was Cabeza de Vaca's.
   b. The first explorer's ship to circumnavigate the world was Ferdinand Magellan's.

4. **a.** Spanish conquistadores were peaceful missionaries.
   b. Spanish conquitadores were violent marauders out for themselves.

5. **a.** Vasco Núñez de Balboa was probably the first European to see the Pacific Ocean.
   b. Vasco Núñez de Balboa was probably the first European to see the Atlantic Ocean.

6. **a.** The Treaty of Tordesillas was signed to end boundary disputes between Spain and Portugal.
   b. The Treaty of Tordesillas was signed to grant Spain the new colonies in South America.

7. **a.** Malintzin provided secret information to Cortés.
   b. Malintzin provided secret information to Pizarro.

8. **a.** Moctezuma encouraged Cortés to come to Tenochtitlán.
   b. Moctezuma tried to bribe Cortés with gold so he would not come to Tenochtitlán.

■■ **POST-READING QUICK CHECK** After you have finished reading the section, in the space provided, list three ways the Catholic religion directly or indirectly affected American Indians.

1. _____

2. _____

3. _____

CHAPTER
2

Empires of the Americas

GUIDED READING STRATEGIES 2.3

■ READING THE SECTION As you read the section, match each of the following terms with the correct definition by writing the letter of the definition in the space provided.

_____ **1.** *audiencia*

_____ **2.** viceroyalties

_____ **3.** missions

_____ **4.** haciendas

_____ **5.** ranchos

_____ **6.** peons

_____ **7.** *peninsulares*

_____ **8.** mestizos

a. Spaniards born in Spain; people at the top of the social structure in Spanish America

b. a form of Spanish settlement with a church at the center; the primary purpose of the settlement was to convert American Indians to Catholicism

c. people born of European-Indian parents

d. smaller farms and ranches formed by the Spanish government

e. people, mostly American Indians, who worked on the haciendas and who owned no land of their own

f. council whose members reported directly and privately to the king of Spain

g. large farming or ranching estates formed by the Spanish government

h. individually governed provinces of the Spanish Empire

■ POST-READING QUICK CHECK After you have finished reading the section, in the space provided, list four territories the Spanish settled in North America. List them in the order in which they were settled, from earliest to latest.

1. _____

2. _____

3. _____

4. _____

CHAPTER 2

Empires of the Americas

GUIDED READING STRATEGIES 2.4

■ **READING THE SECTION** Review the list of events before reading the section. Then as you read the section, number the following events in the order in which they occurred.

_____ **1.** Giovanni da Verrazano claimed land for France along the east coast of North America.

_____ **2.** The Protestant Reformation began in Germany.

_____ **3.** Francis Drake, one of the English "sea dogs," left England with a fleet of ships to explore and to loot Spanish ships in the Americas.

_____ **4.** John Rolfe introduced Caribbean tobacco to Virginia; farmers began cultivating the tobacco and sending it to England.

_____ **5.** The English defeated the Spanish Armada.

_____ **6.** Pocahontas was captured and converted to Christianity.

_____ **7.** King James I issued the Charter of 1606, giving two companies the right to establish settlements and mining operations in Virginia.

_____ **8.** Sir Walter Raleigh sent a small group of colonists to settle Virginia.

_____ **9.** Jamestown, a Virginia settlement near a river along the Chesapeake Bay, was founded.

■ **POST-READING QUICK CHECK** After you have finished reading the section, in the space provided, list four people you consider to be the most important to the events described in Section 4 and explain their significance.

1. Person: _____ Significance: _____

_____

2. Person: _____ Significance: _____

_____

3. Person: _____ Significance: _____

_____

4. Person: _____ Significance: _____

CHAPTER 3 The English Colonies

GUIDED READING STRATEGIES 3.1

■ **READING THE SECTION** Each of the following sentences contains an under-lined word, phrase, or name that makes the sentence incorrect. As you read the section, use the space provided to write the word, phrase, or name that makes the sentence correct.

_____ **1.** Cooperation between the church and state was called the **New World Way**.

_____ **2.** King Henry VIII broke from the **Anglican Church**.

_____ **3.** The founders of the Plymouth colony called themselves **Separatists**.

_____ **4.** The **Roman Catholic Church** was also referred to as the Church of England.

_____ **5.** **The Great Flight** refers to a time when thousands of people fled England to escape religious persecution.

_____ **6.** Minister Thomas Hooker wrote the **Fundamental Orders of Plymouth**, the first written constitution in the colonies.

_____ **7.** Pilgrims signed the **Massachusetts Compact** to establish a self-governing colony.

_____ **8.** Most **men** did not work in the fields, but they did help at harvest time.

■ **POST-READING QUICK CHECK** After you have finished reading the section, in the space provided, list three benefits the Puritans enjoyed after moving to the New England colonies.

1. _____

2. _____

3. _____

CHAPTER 3

The English Colonies

GUIDED READING STRATEGIES 3.2

■■ **READING THE SECTION** As you read the section, complete the graphic organizer by supplying information about society and slavery in the Chesapeake.

Society and Slavery in the Chesapeake

Fact	Significance
More Protestants than Catholics settled in Maryland.	
Farmers in the Chesapeake did not bring their crops to a central market.	
There were indentured servants among the participants in Bacon's Rebellion.	
Expansion of slavery in the Chesapeake gave new life to the slave trade.	

■■ **POST-READING QUICK CHECK** After you have finished reading the section, in the space provided, list three ways the population of the Chesapeake differed from that of New England.

1. _____

2. _____

3. _____

CHAPTER 3 The English Colonies

GUIDED READING STRATEGIES 3.3

■■ **READING THE SECTION** As you read the section, complete the following graphic organizers by supplying information about each of the listed colonies.

The Carolinas

named for _____

colonists: _____

method of making a living:

_____

type of slave system:

_____

Pennsylvania

named for: _____

colonists: _____

method of making a living:

_____

slaves? _____

New York

originally named: _____

colonists: _____

renamed for: _____

method of making a living:

_____

Georgia

founded by: _____

colonists: _____

■■ **POST-READING QUICK CHECK** After you have finished reading the section, in the space provided, explain three provisions of the Navigation Acts.

1. Provision: _____

2. Provision: _____

3. Provision: _____

CHAPTER
3

The English Colonies

GUIDED READING STRATEGIES 3.4

■ **READING THE SECTION** Review the list of events before reading the section. Then as you read the section, number the following events in the order in which they occurred.

_____ 1. The British of Plymouth Colony ended a war with the Pequot by burning a Pequot village, killing hundreds of people.

_____ 2. The British captured Louisburg on Cape Breton Island, which guarded the entrance to the Gulf of St. Lawrence.

_____ 3. The Treaty of Paris was signed.

_____ 4. The French founded New Orleans.

_____ 5. The Iroquois League was formed, including the Cayuga, Mohawk, Oneida, Onondaga, and Seneca peoples.

_____ 6. The French and Indian War began in the colonies.

_____ 7. The British captured Fort Frontenac on Lake Ontario.

_____ 8. The Iroquois League became known as the Six Nations when the Tuscarora joined.

_____ 9. The British took Quebec from the French.

■ **POST-READING QUICK CHECK** After you have finished reading the section, in the space provided, list the three people you consider to be the most important to the events described in Section 4 and explain their significance.

1. Person: _____ Significance: _____

_____

2. Person: _____ Significance: _____

_____

3. Person: _____ Significance: _____

_____

CHAPTER 4 Independence!

GUIDED READING STRATEGIES 4.1

■ **READING THE SECTION** As you read the section, circle the boldface word or phrase that best completes each statement below.

1. War against settlers and the British begun by an Ottowa chief was called **Delaware's Rebellion/Pontiac's Rebellion**.

2. The **Proclamation of 1763/Quartering Act** barred settlement west of the Appalachian Mountains.

3. A tax on imported goods is called a **mark/duty**.

4. **Nonimportation agreements/Importation writs** were signed by colonial merchants to promise not to buy or import British goods.

5. The group of artisans, lawyers, and merchants who joined forces to protest the Stamp Act were called the **Sons of Liberty/Freedom Fighters**.

6. The **Declaratory Act/Deliberative Act** was passed by Parliament in 1766 asserting its right to make laws and bind the colonies.

7. Laws placing taxes on common imported items, like tea, lead, and glass, were called the **Townshend Acts/Declaratory Acts**.

8. **Writs of Search/Writs of Assistance** were general search warrants that allowed customs officers to search vessels, warehouses, or homes even if they only suspected they might contain smuggled goods.

9. The **Housing Act/Quartering Act** was a law that required colonists to house and supply British troops.

10. A clash between British soldiers and colonists that left five colonists dead was called the **Boston Massacre/Pontiac Rebellion**.

■ **POST-READING QUICK CHECK** After you have finished reading the section, in the space provided, explain why many colonists did not feel England had the right to impose taxes on them.

_____

_____

_____

CHAPTER
4

Independence!

GUIDED READING STRATEGIES 4.2

■ **READING THE SECTION** As you read the section, complete the following chart by listing the colonists' point of view and the British point of view for each item.

Points of View

Action	Colonists' Point of View	British Point of View
Tea Act of 1773		
Intolerable Acts of 1774		
First Continental Congress		
Battle for Boston		

■ **POST-READING QUICK CHECK** After you have finished reading the section, in the space provided list three people you consider to be most important to the events in Section 2 and explain their significance.

1. Person: _____ Significance: _____

_____

2. Person: _____ Significance: _____

_____

3. Person: _____ Significance: _____

_____

CHAPTER 4 Independence!

GUIDED READING STRATEGIES 4.3

■■ **READING THE SECTION** As you read the section, complete the following chart by listing people's reactions to the Declaration of Independence.

The Declaration of Independence

Person or People	Reactions

■■ **POST-READING QUICK CHECK** After you have finished reading the section, in the space provided, list the three people you consider to be the most important to the events described in Section 3 and explain their significance.

1. Person: _____ Significance: _____

_____

2. Person: _____ Significance: _____

_____

3. Person: _____ Significance: _____

_____

CHAPTER 4

Independence!

GUIDED READING STRATEGIES 4.4

■ **READING THE SECTION** As you read the section, complete the following outline by supplying the main idea and the missing subtopics and supporting details.

An American Victory

Main Idea: _____

_____

Topic I: After the British evacuation of Boston, George Washington knew the Redcoats would strike again somewhere else.

    Detail A: _____

    Detail B: _____

    Detail C: As the tide turned in the Patriots' favor, European countries and individuals offered troops, supplies, and gold.

Topic II: _____

    Detail A: _____

    Detail B: _____

Topic III: _____

    Detail A: _____

    Detail B: The Treaty of Paris was signed on September 3, 1783.

■ **POST-READING QUICK CHECK** After you have finished reading the section, in the space provided, list four provisions of the Treaty of Paris.

1. Provision: _____

2. Provision: _____

3. Provision: _____

4. Provision: _____

Guided Reading Strategies

From Confederation to Federal Union

GUIDED READING STRATEGIES 5.1

■ **READING THE SECTION** As you read the section, complete the following chart by listing the powers the Articles of Confederation granted to Congress and the powers it did not grant to Congress.

Articles of Confederation

Powers Granted to Congress	Powers Not Granted to Congress
_____	_____
_____	_____
_____	
_____	
_____	
_____	
_____	

■ **POST-READING QUICK CHECK** After you have finished reading the section, in the space provided, list three ways that the concept of Republican Motherhood affected women's lives.

1. Responsibility: _____

2. Responsibility: _____

3. Responsibility: _____

CHAPTER 5 From Confederation to Federal Union

GUIDED READING STRATEGIES 5.2

■ READING THE SECTION As you read the section, complete the following chart by explaining the major compromises made in the drafting of the Constitution.

The Constitution

Compromise	Explanation
The Great Compromise	_____ _____ _____ _____ _____ _____
The Three-Fifths Compromise	_____ _____
Compromise on Tariffs	_____ _____ _____ _____
Compromise on Slavery	_____ _____

■ POST-READING QUICK CHECK After you have finished reading the section, in the space provided, list three reasons for opposition to ratification of the Constitution.

1. Reason: _____

2. Reason: _____

3. Reason: _____

▌▌**READING THE SECTION** As you read the section, complete the following outline by supplying the main idea and the missing subtopics and supporting details.

The Constitution: A Living Document

Main Idea: _____

Topic I: The Constitution was designed to have a strong central government that also safeguards states' rights.

    Detail A: _____

    Detail B: _____

    Detail C: Concurrent powers are powers held jointly by the state and federal governments.

    Detail D: _____

Topic II: _____

    Detail A: The checks and balances system gives each branch of government the power to restrain the other two.

    Detail B: _____

    Detail C: _____

    Detail D: Congress has the power to override a presidential veto.

    Detail E: _____

Topic III: _____

    Detail A: The Constitution can be kept current by the writing of new amendments.

    Detail B: _____

▌▌**POST-READING QUICK CHECK** After you have finished reading the section, in the space provided, give three examples of the "checks and balances" built into the Constitution. Be sure to include all three branches of government.

    1. _____

    2. _____

    3. _____

CHAPTER 6 A Strong Start for the Nation

GUIDED READING STRATEGIES 6.1

■ **READING THE SECTION** Each of the following sentences contains an underlined word, phrase, or name that makes the sentence incorrect. As you read the section, use the space provided to write the word, phrase, or name that makes the sentence correct.

_____ 1. The Judiciary Act of 1789 established a federal district court for each <u>village</u>.

_____ 2. The president's advisers came to be known as his <u>court</u>.

_____ 3. The financial proposals of <u>John Adams</u> were often controversial.

_____ 4. An economic system based on a free market and private ownership is called <u>communism</u>.

_____ 5. The philosophy of strict interpretation of the Constitution is called <u>literal construction</u>.

_____ 6. Believing the government can do anything the Constitution does not specifically forbid is called <u>free construction</u>.

_____ 7. The <u>Quaker</u> Rebellion, in which a group of farmers were protesting a new tax, was a challenge to federal authority.

_____ 8. The Treaty of Greenville gave the United States title to much of the land that now makes up present-day <u>Maryland</u>.

■ **POST-READING QUICK CHECK** After you have finished reading, list and briefly explain three conflicts that took place on the American frontier during the time period discussed in Section 1.

1. _____

_____

2. _____

_____

3. _____

_____

CHAPTER 6 A Strong Start for the Nation

GUIDED READING STRATEGIES 6.2

■ **READING THE SECTION** As you read the section, examine the riddles below. Solve each riddle by writing the correct name or term in the space provided.

_____ 1. "I am a young French diplomat who encouraged Americans to aid France."

_____ 2. "I will not seek a third term."

_____ 3. "I created the Navy Department and strengthened the army."

_____ 4. "After I was signed, the British abandoned their forts in the Northwest Territory."

_____ 5. "I included angry mobs, beheadings, and the storming of the Bastille."

_____ 6. "I am the incident that made the American people furious with France."

_____ 7. "We gave the president the power to expel all dangerous foreigners from the United States and imprison all Americans who wrote false or malicious statements against the U.S. government."

_____ 8. "I was a way for the British to kidnap American sailors and make them work on British ships."

■ **POST-READING QUICK CHECK** After you have finished reading the section, in the space provided, briefly explain the leaders, the supporters, and the views of the Federalist Party and the Democratic-Republican Party.

1. Federalist Party: _____

_____

2. Democratic-Republican Party: _____

_____

CHAPTER 6 — A Strong Start for the Nation

GUIDED READING STRATEGIES 6.3

■ **READING THE SECTION** As you read the section, match each of the following people with the correct description by writing the letter of the description in the space provided.

_____ **1.** Aaron Burr

_____ **2.** John Marshall

_____ **3.** Toussaint-Louverture

_____ **4.** Meriwether Lewis

_____ **5.** Sacagawea

_____ **6.** Zebulon Pike

a. woman who served as guide and interpreter on the expedition to map the Louisiana Territory

b. leader of the African slave revolt in Saint Domingue

c. explorer who was the first to describe to Americans the lands west of the Mississippi

d. Chief Justice of the United States, chosen by President Adams

e. one of two men that President Jefferson asked to map the Louisiana Territory

f. Republican who tied with Jefferson in electoral votes for president during the election of 1800

■ **POST-READING QUICK CHECK** After you have finished reading the section, in the space provided, list three reasons France sold the United States all of the Louisiana Territory.

1. _____

2. _____

3. _____

CHAPTER 6

A Strong Start for the Nation

GUIDED READING STRATEGIES 6.4

■ **READING THE SECTION** As you read the section, circle the boldface word or phrase that best completes each statement below.

1. The British passed the **Embargo Act/Orders in Council** to stop neutral vessels from trading with France.

2. Congress passed the **Embargo Act/Shipping Act** to stop the shipping of American products to all foreign ports.

3. All American trade with Britain and France was prohibited by the **Non-Intercourse Act/ Non-Trading Act**.

4. At the Battle of Tippecanoe, **Tecumseh/General William Henry Harrison** was defeated.

5. The British hold on the Northwest Territory was broken by their loss at the **Battle of New Orleans/Battle of the Thames**.

6. America's most decisive victory in the War of 1812 was the **Battle of the Thames/Battle of New Orleans**.

7. The War of 1812 ended with the signing of the **Treaty of Ghent/Hartford Treaty**.

8. At the **Hartford Convention/Convention of Thames**, many Americans pushed for secession from the Union.

■ **POST-READING QUICK CHECK** After you have finished reading the section, list three reasons for the War of 1812.

1. _____

2. _____

3. _____

CHAPTER 7 Nationalism and Economic Growth

GUIDED READING STRATEGIES 7.1

■ **READING THE SECTION** Review the list of events before reading the section. Then as you read the section, number the following events in the order in which they occurred.

_____ **1.** The United States and Britain signed the Rush-Bagot Agreement, which limited each country's naval presence on the Great Lakes.

_____ **2.** In his annual message to Congress, President Monroe said that the United States would not interfere with any existing European colonies in Latin America but that the United States would consider it "dangerous to our peace and safety" if any European country tried to regain a former colony or establish a new colony in the Western Hemisphere.

_____ **3.** Republican James Monroe was elected president.

_____ **4.** Secretary of State Adams warned Russia that the United States would not tolerate any new colonies on the American continents.

_____ **5.** General Andrew Jackson became commander of a force to stop Indian raids in East Florida. The conflict became known as the First Seminole War.

_____ **6.** President Monroe wrote a letter to Thomas Jefferson, in which he wrote, "We would view an interference [in Latin America] on the part of the European powers as an attack on ourselves."

_____ **7.** Britain and the United States agreed to share fishing rights in the waters between the United States and Canada.

_____ **8.** Spain ceded East Florida to the United States because Spain could not guarantee they could control the Seminole, who had been attacking nearby U.S. towns.

■ **POST-READING QUICK CHECK** After you have finished reading the section, in the space provided, briefly explain why the period immediately following the War of 1812 was referred to as the Era of Good Feelings.

_____

_____

_____

Guided Reading Strategies

Nationalism and Economic Growth

GUIDED READING STRATEGIES 7.2

■ **READING THE SECTION** As you read the section, examine each pair of statements below. Circle the letter of the statement in each pair that is true.

1. **a.** A chain reaction of bank failures, falling land prices, and foreclosures in 1819 was called the Great Depression.
   b. A chain reaction of bank failures, falling land prices, and foreclosures in 1819 was called the Panic of 1819.

2. **a.** A roadway that connected the eastern and western territories was called the National Road.
   b. A roadway that connected the eastern and western territories was called the Western Way.

3. **a.** Specie was American money that could be traded for gold in England.
   b. Specie was gold or silver coins.

4. **a.** A reorganization of the production process that allowed the manufacture of large quantities of goods was called the Market Revolution.
   b. A reorganization of the production process that allowed the manufacture of large quantities of goods was called the Industrial Revolution.

5. **a.** The American System was Henry Clay's idea for more federal involvement in the economy.
   b. The Tariff Act was Henry Clay's idea for more federal involvement in the economy.

6. **a.** The Erie Canal was built to link the New York River with Lake Erie.
   b. The Erie Canal was built to link the Hudson River with Lake Erie.

7. **a.** The manufacturing of large quantities of goods was called mass marketing.
   b. The manufacturing of large quantities of goods was called mass production.

8. **a.** Improvements in transportation helped manufacturers because their goods could be shipped cheaper and faster.
   b. Improvements in transportation hurt manufacturers because their goods were shipped to market too quickly for buyers.

■ **POST-READING QUICK CHECK** After you have finished reading the section, in the space provided, list three improvements in transportation that took place during the time period discussed in Section 2.

1. _____

2. _____

3. _____

Nationalism and Economic Growth

GUIDED READING STRATEGIES 7.3

■ READING THE SECTION As you read the section, complete the following chart by explaining the ways in which Jacksonian Democracy broke with the past.

Jacksonian Democracy

Change	Explanation
the presidential campaign	
changes in voting rights	
the spoils system	
government reform	

■ POST-READING QUICK CHECK After you have finished reading the section, in the space provided, explain the Missouri Compromise.

_____

_____

_____

CHAPTER 7 Nationalism and Economic Growth

GUIDED READING STRATEGIES 7.4

■ **READING THE SECTION** As you read the section, examine the riddles below.
Solve each riddle by writing the correct name or term in the space provided.

_____ 1. "I was passed because white settlers wanted more and more lands for settlement."

_____ 2. "I started when American Indians violently refused their removal orders."

_____ 3. "I limited state power over Indian lands."

_____ 4. "I am the forced removal of the Cherokee from their lands in the east."

_____ 5. "In my opinion, states have the right to disobey any act of Congress they think is unconstitutional."

_____ 6. "I began when a run on American banks coincided with an economic crisis in Great Britain."

_____ 7. "I am an order instructing the Treasury to accept only gold or silver as payment for public land."

■ **POST-READING QUICK CHECK** After you have finished reading the section,
list three ways the Cherokee attempted to adapt to white culture.

1. _____

2. _____

3. _____

Regional Societies

GUIDED READING STRATEGIES 8.1

■ **READING THE SECTION** As you read the section, examine each pair of statements below. Circle the letter of the statement in each pair that is true.

1. **a.** In the mid-1800s middle-class children typically had to work long hours to help pay for family expenses.
   b. In the mid-1800s middle-class children typically did not have to work to help support their families.

2. **a.** There was a vast difference between the way that wealthy and poor people lived.
   b. There was very little difference between the way that wealthy and poor people lived.

3. **a.** The town of Boston, Massachusetts, changed its name to Lowell in honor of the man who constructed and designed a power loom for a factory.
   b. The town of Waltham, Massachusetts, changed its name to Lowell in honor of the man who constructed and designed a power loom for a factory.

4. **a.** From the 1830s to the 1850s, vandals often attacked Protestant schools.
   b. From the 1830s to the 1850s, vandals often attacked Catholic schools.

5. **a.** Millions of men and women who left Ireland because of famine came to the United States and discovered that they were discriminated against.
   b. Millions of men and women who left Germany because of famine came to the United States and discovered that they were discriminated against.

6. **a.** Because of the demand of city dwellers for food, the United States went through a market revolution.
   b. Because of the demand of city dwellers for food, the United States developed a nativist economy.

7. **a.** One tactic used by labor unions to help raise workers' wages was to increase productivity.
   b. One tactic used by labor unions to help raise workers' wages was the strike.

8. **a.** The most important reason for Europeans to migrate to the United States was the possibility of choosing which religion to follow.
   b. The most important reason for Europeans to migrate to the United States was the possibility of economic opportunity.

■ **POST-READING QUICK CHECK** After you have finished reading the section, describe the housing and living conditions of the wealthy, the middle class, and the poor in the North.

1. Wealthy _____

2. Middle Class _____

3. Poor _____

CHAPTER 8 Regional Societies

GUIDED READING STRATEGIES 8.2

■ READING THE SECTION Each of the following sentences contains an under-
lined word or phrase that makes the sentence incorrect. As you read the section, write
the word or phrase that makes the sentence correct.

_____ 1. The class structure of the prerevolutionary South reflected how important both land and slaves were.

_____ 2. Nearly half of the 260,000 free African Americans lived in the Lower South.

_____ 3. African Americans justified their position in society by saying that the Bible said that they were superior to other races.

_____ 4. Cotton production in the South soared after the introduction of the steamboat.

_____ 5. The group ranked the highest in the social order in the South were the yeoman farmers.

_____ 6. The most important food crop in the South was fruit because there was plenty of it and it could be cooked in a number of ways.

_____ 7. African Americans, European Americans, and American Indians all contributed to the art of making armaments.

_____ 8. The most important cash crop in the South was tobacco.

■ POST-READING QUICK CHECK After you have finished reading the section,
summarize what it was like to be a "free" African American in the time period discussed in Section 2.

_____

_____

_____

CHAPTER 8 Regional Societies

GUIDED READING STRATEGIES 8.3

■ **READING THE SECTION** As you read the section, complete the following chart by briefly explaining the characteristics of slave existence in the 1800s.

Slave Existence in the 1800s

Area of Life	Characteristics
Jobs	
Housing	
Treatment by owners	
Music	
Religion	

■ **POST-READING QUICK CHECK** After you have finished reading the section, explain how the Underground Railroad worked.

_____

_____

_____

Working for Reform

GUIDED READING STRATEGIES 9.1

■■■**READING THE SECTION** As you read the section, circle the boldface word or phrase that best completes each statement below.

1. **Ralph Waldo Emerson/Charles Grandison Finney** was a white traveling revival minister who delivered hundreds of sermons in the 1820s and 1830s.

2. A Methodist African American woman, **Mother Ann Lee/Jarena Lee,** traveled hundreds of miles to preach to both black and white worshippers.

3. **Richard Allen/Mother Ann Lee** was the founder of the Bethel African Methodist Episcopal Church.

4. The leader of the Shakers was **Mother Ann Lee/Jarena Lee,** who claimed to be the messiah who would found a sinless society.

5. **Joseph Smith/Brigham Young** started the Mormons, or Church of Jesus Christ of Latter-Day Saints.

6. The Mormons were led out of Illinois to successful settlements in the Great Salt Lake Valley by **Brigham Young/Joseph Smith.**

7. A member of the transcendentalist movement, **Charles Grandison Finney/Ralph Waldo Emerson** was a prominent writer.

8. The utopian community Brook Farm was formed by **George Ripley/Richard Allen,** a Unitarian minister.

■■■**POST-READING QUICK CHECK** After you have finished reading the section, list three beliefs that the philosophy of transcendentalism promoted.

1. _____

2. _____

3. _____

CHAPTER 9 Working for Reform

GUIDED READING STRATEGIES 9.2

■ **READING THE SECTION** As you read the section, complete the graphic organizer by supplying the missing information about each of the types of social reform discussed in Section 2.

Movements for Social Reform

Type of reform: Temperance **Key reformer(s):** _____ _____ **Accomplishments:** _____ _____ _____ _____	**Type of reform:** College **Key reformer(s):** _____ **Accomplishments:** _____ _____ _____	**Type of reform:** Women's education **Key reformer(s):** _____ _____ **Accomplishments:** _____ _____ _____
	Type of reform: _____ **Key reformer(s):** Josiah Quincy **Accomplishments:** _____ _____ _____	
Type of reform: _____ **Key reformer(s):** Horace Mann **Accomplishments:** _____ _____ _____	**Type of reform:** The poor **Key reformer(s):** none **Accomplishments:** _____ _____ _____	**Type of reform:** _____ _____ **Key reformer(s):** Dorthea Dix **Accomplishments:** _____ _____ _____

■ **POST-READING QUICK CHECK** After you have finished reading the section, in the space provided, list three reasons women became involved in reform in the period discussed in Section 2.

1. Reason: _____

2. Reason: _____

3. Reason: _____

CHAPTER 9 **Working for Reform**

GUIDED READING STRATEGIES 9.3

■ **READING THE SECTION** As you read the section, complete the following outline by supplying the main idea and the missing subtopics and supporting details.

The Crusade for Abolition

Main Idea: _____

Topic I: _____

        Detail A: _____

        Detail B: Most African Americans rejected the move for colonization.

Topic II: Abolitionists called for the immediate end to slavery.

        Detail A: _____

Topic III: _____

        Detail A: The American Anti-Slavery Society was formed to fight for abolition and racial equality.

        Detail B: _____

        Detail C: _____

        Detail D: _____

Topic IV: The abolition movement began to encounter problems.

        Detail A: _____

        Detail B: _____

■ **POST-READING QUICK CHECK** After you have finished reading the section, briefly explain the ways that African Americans changed the focus from colonization of freed slaves to abolition of slavery.

_____

_____

_____

CHAPTER 9 Working for Reform

GUIDED READING STRATEGIES 9.4

■ **READING THE SECTION** As you read the section, complete the graphic organizers by answering the five W's.

Seneca Falls Convention	Declaration of Sentiments	Married Women's Property Act
What?	What?	What?
When?	When?	When?
Where?	Where?	Where?
Who?	Who?	Who?
Why?	Why?	Why?

■ **POST-READING QUICK CHECK** After you have finished reading the section, list three of the issues the leaders of the women's rights movement addressed.

1. _____

2. _____

3. _____

Expansion and Conflict

GUIDED READING STRATEGIES 10.1

■ **READING THE SECTION** As you read the section, complete the graphic organizers by supplying the missing information about each of these important battles of the Texas Revolution. The graphic organizers are arranged in chronological order.

Major Battles of the Texas Revolution

Battle: The Alamo

When occurred: _____

Major leaders: _____

Outcome: _____

Significance: _____

Battle: _____

When occurred: _____

Outcome: Mexican troops defeated rebel army and about 400 surviving Texans surrendered; Santa Anna ordered that prisoners be executed for treason

Significance: _____

Battle: _____

When occurred: April 21, 1836

Major leaders: _____

Outcome: _____

Significance: _____

■ **POST-READING QUICK CHECK** After you have finished reading the section, in the space provided, write a brief summary comparing and contrasting the ideas that different Americans had concerning the idea of manifest destiny.

_____

_____

Expansion and Conflict

GUIDED READING STRATEGIES 10.2

■ **READING THE SECTION** As you read the section, match each of the following people with the correct description by writing the letter of the description in the space provided.

_____ **1.** James K. Polk

_____ **2.** Juan Cortina

_____ **3.** Zachary Taylor

_____ **4.** Winfield Scott

_____ **5.** Henry Clay

_____ **6.** John Slidell

_____ **7.** James Gadsden

_____ **8.** Stephen Kearny

_____ **9.** John C. Frémont

_____ **10.** John Sloat

a. Louisiana lawyer sent by President Polk to negotiate for the United States in Mexico City in 1845

b. U.S. general who led troops into the Rio Grande region in 1845, which led to the start of the Mexican War

c. former governor of Tennessee who served as president of the United States from 1845 to 1849

d. commodore in the U.S. Marines who, in July 1846, led troops to capture Monterey, California

e. member of a prominent Tejano family in South Texas who headed a rebellion against white discrimination

f. U.S. diplomat who negotiated a deal with Mexico to secure an additional strip of land south of the Gila River

g. U.S. general who led the siege of Mexico City

h. Whig Party candidate who ran against James K. Polk in the 1844 presidential election

i. U.S. officer who led the Bear Flag Revolt in California in 1846

j. U.S. brigadier general who, in 1846, led an army that seized New Mexico

■ **POST-READING QUICK CHECK** After you have finished reading the section, in the space provided, write some examples of how the Mexican War was viewed by some as "Mr. Polk's War."

_____

_____

_____

_____

_____

Expansion and Conflict

GUIDED READING STRATEGIES 10.3

■ **READING THE SECTION** As you read the section, complete the following outline by supplying the main idea and the missing subtopics and supporting details.

The Far West

Main Idea: Many Americans traveled west for new lives and greater opportunities.

Topic I: _____

    Detail A: The 780-mile-long Santa Fe Trail became a major route and stopping point to the West for many Americans.

    Detail B: _____

    Detail C: _____

Topic II: The opening of the Oregon Trail led many Americans to travel west, causing conflicts with other groups.

    Detail A: _____

    Detail B: _____

Topic III: During the 1840s and 1850s, thousands of Americans traveled the Oregon Trail.

    Detail A: _____

    Detail B: _____

    Detail C: _____

    Detail D: _____

    Detail E: The Treaty of Fort Laramie was produced to settle disputes between western settlers and Great Plains Indians.

Topic IV: In the Oregon Country, conflicts between settlers and American Indians continued.

    Detail A: _____

Topic V: _____

    Detail A: By 1860 some 40,000 Mormons had arrived, most of them living in the Great Salt Lake area.

    Detail B: _____

■ **POST-READING QUICK CHECK** After you have finished reading the section, in the space provided, list the starting and ending points of the Santa Fe Trail and the Oregon Trail.

1. Santa Fe Trail: _____

2. Oregon Trail: _____

CHAPTER 10 Expansion and Conflict

GUIDED READING STRATEGIES 10.4

■ **READING THE SECTION** Review the list of events before reading the section. Then as you read the section, number the folowing events in the order in which they occurred.

_____ 1. The Mexican government begins to transfer ownership of mission lands to the Californios.

_____ 2. Americans on the East Coast hear of the gold in California.

_____ 3. President Polk confirms the account of gold in California in a message to Congress.

_____ 4. Spain begins to establish communities in California.

_____ 5. Thousands of Americans, Mexicans, and South Americans make their way to the goldfields of California.

_____ 6. Some Californios are first to reach the goldfields and to make the first major gold strikes.

_____ 7. Gold seekers from as far away as Australia, China, and Europe rush to the goldfields of California.

_____ 8. James W. Marshall detects flecks of gold in the bottom of a wooden canal on Sutter's land.

_____ 9. The resulting international mix of gold seekers diversifies the population of California.

_____ 10. Augustus Sutter arrives from Switzerland and establishes a fort and trading post on the California Trail.

■ **POST-READING QUICK CHECK** After you have finished reading the section, in the space provided, explain how each of the following groups affected the American Indian population in California during this period.

1. Spanish settlers (Californios): _____

_____

_____

_____

2. Forty-niners: _____

_____

Sectional Conflict Increases

GUIDED READING STRATEGIES 11.1

■ **READING THE SECTION** As you read the section, match each of the descriptions with the name of the person being described by writing the correct letter in the space provided.

_____ **1.** The Senator who proposed, along with Lewis Cass, the concept of popular sovereignty was
   a. David Wilmot.
   b. Stephen Douglas.
   c. Zachary Taylor.
   d. Henry Clay.

_____ **2.** The Representative who introduced an amendment that would ban slavery in all lands that would be acquired from Mexico was
   a. David Wilmot.
   b. Martin Van Buren.
   c. Henry Clay.
   d. John C. Calhoun.

_____ **3.** The democratic presidential candidate in the election of 1848 was
   a. Zachary Taylor.
   b. Martin Van Buren.
   c. Lewis Cass.
   d. Millard Fillmore.

_____ **4.** The presidential candidate for the Free-Soil Party in the election of 1848 was
   a. Millard Fillmore.
   b. Zachary Taylor.
   c. Lewis Cass.
   d. Martin Van Buren.

_____ **5.** A veteran leader of the Whigs was
   a. Daniel Webster.
   b. Stephen Douglas.
   c. Lewis Cass.
   d. David Wilmot.

_____ **6.** The elder statesman who advocated compromise between northern and southern interests was
   a. John C. Calhoun.
   b. Henry Clay.
   c. Robert Barnwell Rhett.
   d. Stephen Douglas.

_____ **7.** The elder statesman from the South who advocated a dual presidency was
   a. David Wilmot.
   b. Lewis Cass.
   c. John C. Calhoun.
   d. Millard Fillmore.

_____ **8.** The Fire-eater who represented the South in Congress was
   a. Martin Van Buren.
   b. Henry Clay.
   c. Millard Fillmore.
   d. Robert Barnwell Rhett.

■ **POST-READING QUICK CHECK** After you have finished reading the section, in the space provided, explain why the Free-Soil Party was formed.

_____

_____

Sectional Conflict Increases

GUIDED READING STRATEGIES 11.2

CHAPTER 11

■ **READING THE SECTION** Preview the list below. Then, as you read the section, number the following events in the order in which they occurred.

_____ **1.** The Republican Party is formed from antislavery Whigs and Democrats.

_____ **2.** Kansas was admitted into the union as a free state.

_____ **3.** The Kansas-Nebraska Act was passed, organizing the two territories on the basis of popular sovereignty.

_____ **4.** The Fugitive Slave Act made many northerners confront the horrors of slavery.

_____ **5.** Kansas violence between pro-slavery and antislavery groups broke out, leading to the Pottawatomie Massacre.

_____ **6.** The publication of _Uncle Tom's Cabin_ began to change public opinion on slavery.

_____ **7.** The Lecompton Constitution was passed in Kansas, safeguarding the rights of slave-holders there.

_____ **8.** Pro-slavery senator Andrew Butler severely beat abolitionist senator Charles Sumner with a cane.

_____ **9.** Pro-slavery voters used illegal election tactics to elect a pro-slavery legislature in Kansas, angering antislavery crusaders.

_____ **10.** James Buchanan of Pennsylvania was elected president.

_____ **11.** Franklin Pierce won the presidency by persuading people on both sides of the slavery issue that he supported their views.

_____ **12.** Two rival governments began to operate in Kansas.

_____ **13.** New Englanders encouraged antislavery settlers to move to Kansas, while southerners encouraged pro-slavery settlers to move there.

■ **POST-READING QUICK CHECK** After you have finished reading the section, in the space provided, tell who Frederick Douglass was and what he thought of the Fugitive Slave Act.

_____

_____

_____

Sectional Conflict Increases

CHAPTER 11

GUIDED READING STRATEGIES 11.3

■ **READING THE SECTION** As you read the section, match each of the following people with the correct description by writing the letter of the description in the space provided.

_____ 1. Abraham Lincoln

_____ 2. John Brown

_____ 3. Robert E. Lee

_____ 4. John Emerson

_____ 5. Dred Scott

_____ 6. Stephen Douglas

_____ 7. John Bell

_____ 8. Jefferson Davis

_____ 9. John Breckinridge

_____ 10. Roger B. Taney

a. chief justice of the U.S. Supreme Court who wrote the majority opinion against Dred Scott

b. Republican who won the bid for U.S. president in the election of 1860

c. U.S. colonel who led the assault on John Brown and his followers at Harpers Ferry

d. presidential candidate for the Constitutional Union Party in the election of 1860

e. former U.S. senator and secretary of war chosen as provisional president of the Confederacy in 1861

f. slave who sued for his freedom and had his case go to the U.S. Supreme Court in 1856

g. army surgeon who was the owner of slave Dred Scott

h. presidential candidate for the southern Democrats in the election of 1860

i. U.S. senator who strongly supported the policy of popular sovereignty

j. abolitionist who led an attack on a federal arsenal in Harpers Ferry in 1859

■ **POST-READING QUICK CHECK** After you have finished reading the section, in the space provided, write two key ways in which the new constitution for the Confederate States of America was different from the U.S. Constitution.

1. _____

2. _____

CHAPTER
12

The Civil War

GUIDED READING STRATEGIES 12.1

■ **READING THE SECTION** As you read the section, complete the outline by supplying the missing information.

I. Last attempts at compromising with the secessionists

   A. _____

   B. Lincoln's _____

II. The Civil War begins

   A. Attack on _____

      1. _____ victory

III. First battle of the Civil War

   A. First Battle of _____ (Battle of _____)

      1. _____ victory

IV. Organization of the armies

   A. _____ forces

      1. _____ named to head Union forces

   B. _____ forces

      1. _____ named to command the Army of Northern Virginia

      2. _____ named as military adviser

■ **POST-READING QUICK CHECK** After you have finished reading the section, in the space provided, name the four slave states that remained within the Union at the start of the Civil War.

1. _____

2. _____

3. _____

4. _____

CHAPTER 12 The Civil War

GUIDED READING STRATEGIES 12.2

■ **READING THE SECTION** As you read the section, complete the following chart by listing two reasons why people in the South were opposed to the Civil War and three reasons why people in the North were opposed to it.

Opposition to the Civil War

By the South	By the North
1. _____ _____ _____ _____ _____ 2. _____ _____ _____	1. _____ _____ 2. _____ _____ _____ 3. _____ _____

■ **POST-READING QUICK CHECK** After you have finished reading the section, in the space provided, list three reasons why neither France nor Great Britain came to the aid of the South as the South had strategized.

1. _____
_____

2. _____
_____

3. _____
_____

CHAPTER 12

The Civil War

GUIDED READING STRATEGIES 12.3

■ **READING THE SECTION** As you read the section, examine the riddles below. Solve each riddle by writing the correct name or term in the space provided.

_____ 1. "I am the famous regiment that included African American troops."

_____ 2. "My hesitancy angered President Lincoln."

_____ 3. "I refused to order my Union forces to retreat at Shiloh. And I made the right call."

_____ 4. "Whoever controlled me controlled the Mississippi River."

_____ 5. "I am the Union general who led my men across an open field at Fredericksburg."

_____ 6. "I led the Confederate armies at the Battle of Antietam."

_____ 7. "My own men shot me by mistake at Chancellorsville."

_____ 8. "I led an army of 13,000 Confederates at Yorktown."

■ **POST-READING QUICK CHECK** After you have finished reading the section, in the space provided, summarize what Lincoln's Emancipation Proclamation stated and when it took effect.

_____

_____

_____

_____

_____

_____

_____

_____

_____

_____

CHAPTER 12 The Civil War

GUIDED READING STRATEGIES 12.4

■ READING THE SECTION As you read the section, examine each pair of statements below. Circle the letter of the statement in each pair that is true.

1. **a.** Gettysburg is the town where two Union brigades surprised a Confederate raiding party on July 1, 1863.
   b. Richmond is the town where two Union brigades surprised a Confederate raiding party on July 1, 1863.

2. **a.** General Joseph Johnston surrendered to General William Tecumseh Sherman at Appomattox Courthouse.
   b. General Joseph Johnston surrendered to General William Tecumseh Sherman at Durham Station.

3. **a.** President Lincoln told General Grant that his goal was for the Union army to march on Gettysburg.
   b. President Lincoln told General Grant that his goal was for the Union army to march on Richmond.

4. **a.** After capturing Atlanta, Sherman's troops set fire to large portions of it.
   b. After capturing New Orleans, Sherman's troops set fire to large portions of it.

5. **a.** General Grant and his troops laid siege to the Mississippi River town of New Orleans for six weeks.
   b. General Grant and his troops laid siege to the Mississippi River town of Vicksburg for six weeks.

6. **a.** General Robert E. Lee surrendered to Grant on April 9, 1865, at Spotsylvania Courthouse.
   b. General Robert E. Lee surrendered to Grant on April 9, 1865, at Appomattox Courthouse.

7. **a.** After Grant's promotion to commander of all Union forces, his troops had their first encounter with Confederate troops at Vicksburg.
   b. After Grant's promotion to commander of all Union forces, his troops had their first encounter with Confederate troops at Chancellorsville.

8. **a.** General Sherman gave President Lincoln the city of Savannah as a "Christmas gift."
   b. General Sherman gave President Lincoln the city of Atlanta as a "Christmas gift."

■ POST-READING QUICK CHECK After you have finished reading the section, in the space provided, explain why it was so important to the Union forces to have control over the Mississippi River.

_____

_____

_____

Reconstruction and the New South

GUIDED READING STRATEGIES 13.1

■ **READING THE SECTION** Each of the following sentences contains an under-
lined word, name, or phrase that makes the sentence incorrect. As you read the section, use the space provided to write the word, phrase, or name that makes the
sentence correct.

_____ 1. June 19, 1865, was called <u>Freedom Day</u> and celebrated by many
African Americans across the South.

_____ 2. All southerners who swore allegiance to the Union and promised to abide by the federal antislavery laws would be granted
<u>reinstatement</u>.

_____ 3. The rebuilding of the Confederate states and reuniting of the
nation was called <u>Reunification</u>.

_____ 4. President Lincoln was assassinated by <u>Andrew Johnson</u> on April
14, 1865.

_____ 5. Former Confederate states passed laws called Black Codes to
<u>increase</u> the freedoms of former slaves.

_____ 6. The <u>Anti-Slavery Act</u> banned slavery in America.

_____ 7. President Lincoln was buried in his home state of <u>Ohio</u>.

_____ 8. <u>Ulysses S. Grant</u> became president after Lincoln was assassinated.

■ **POST-READING QUICK CHECK** After you have finished reading the section, in
the space below, tell how most African Americans reacted to the Black Codes.

_____

_____

_____

_____

_____

_____

_____

Reconstruction and the New South

GUIDED READING STRATEGIES 13.2

■ READING THE SECTION As you read the section, consider each of the provisions stated below. In the space provided, write *14* if the provision is covered by the Fourteenth Amendment, write *15* if the provision is covered by the Fifteenth Amendment, or write *No* if the provision is not covered by either amendment.

_____ **1.** Gave African Americans the right to hold office

_____ **2.** Denies states the right to deprive anyone of "life, liberty, or property without due process of law"

_____ **3.** Reduced the number of representatives a state could send to Congress based on how many of the state's male citizens were denied the right to vote

_____ **4.** Stated that "The right of citizens of the United States to vote shall not be denied or abridged by the United States or by any state on account of race, color, or previous condition of servitude"

_____ **5.** Extends equal citizenship to African Americans and all people "born or naturalized in the United States"

_____ **6.** Prevented states from limiting voting rights through discriminatory requirements

_____ **7.** Promised all citizens "equal protection of the laws"

_____ **8.** Gave women the right to vote

■ POST-READING QUICK CHECK After you have finished reading the section, in the space provided, first state the three reasons the House gave for trying to impeach President Johnson in 1868, and then state the three actual grievances the Radical Republicans had against President Johnson.

Reasons given by the House for the impeachment of President Johnson:

1. _____

2. _____

3. _____

Radical Republican grievances against President Johnson:

4. _____

5. _____

6. _____

CHAPTER 13 Reconstruction and the New South

GUIDED READING STRATEGIES 13.3

■ **READING THE SECTION** As you read the section, circle the boldface word or phrase that best completes each statement below.

1. The **Panic of 1873/Poverty of 1874** was a severe economic depression that occurred in the 1870s.

2. The **Empowerment Acts/Enforcement Acts** were passed in 1870 and 1871 to stop violence against African Americans.

3. The deal struck between Republicans and southern Democrats after the election of 1876 was called the **New Agreement/Compromise of 1877**.

4. **Redeemers/Leaders** were supporters of white-controlled governments.

5. Businesses that served the public could not discriminate against African Americans after the **Civil Rights Act of 1875/Enforcement Act** was passed by Congress.

6. Supporters of Reconstruction and the Union cause, **mugwumps/scalawags** were southern whites looked down upon by racist southerners.

7. The **Ku Klux Klan/Scalawags** was a secret terrorist group that targeted African Americans and Republican leaders.

8. White and African American northern Republicans who participated in state political conventions in the South were called **Redeemers/Carpetbaggers**.

■ **POST-READING QUICK CHECK** After you have finished reading the section, in the space provided, state the two key provisions that the Democrats and Republicans agreed to with the Compromise of 1877.

1. _____

_____

2. _____

_____

Reconstruction and the New South

GUIDED READING STRATEGIES 13.4

■ **READING THE SECTION** As you read the section, complete the following outline by supplying the main idea and the missing subtopics and supporting details.

The New South

Main Idea: _____

Topic I: _____

Detail A: Some farmers used the sharecropping system to solve their labor shortage problem.

Detail B: _____

Detail C: _____

Topic II: _____

Detail A: Literacy tests were used to keep African Americans from voting.

Detail B: _____

Detail C: _____

Detail D: The Supreme Court upheld segregation in *Plessy* v. *Ferguson*.

Topic III: Life in the South was changing for African Americans.

Detail A: _____

Detail B: _____

Topic IV: African Americans differed in how to respond to discrimination.

Detail A: Ida B. Wells believed African Americans should protest their unfair treatment.

Detail B: _____

■ **POST-READING QUICK CHECK** After you have finished reading the section, in the space provided, state two ways that southern legislatures attempted to deprive African Americans of the right to vote.

1. _____

2. _____

The Western Crossroads

GUIDED READING STRATEGIES 14.1

■ **READING THE SECTION** As you read the section, complete the graphic organizers by supplying missing information about each of the important confrontations between the American Indians and the United States discussed in Section 1.

Confrontation:	Confrontation:	Confrontation:
_____ _____	_____ _____	_____ _____
Date: 1864	**Date:** June 25, 1876	**Date:** _____
American Indian Leader: Black Kettle	**American Indian Leader:** _____	**American Indian Leader:** _____
U.S. Military Leader: _____	**U.S. Military Leader:** George Armstrong Custer	**U.S. Military Leader:** James Forsyth
Immediate Result: _____ _____	**Immediate Result:** _____ _____	**Immediate Result:** _____ _____
Long Term Result: _____ _____ _____	**Long Term Result:** _____ _____ _____	**Long Term Result:** _____ _____ _____

■ **POST-READING QUICK CHECK** After you have finished reading the section, explain how the three people listed were important to the events described in Section 1.

1. Wovoka   Significance: _____

2. Chief Joseph   Significance: _____

3. Sarah Winnemucca   Significance: _____

CHAPTER 14 The Western Crossroads

GUIDED READING STRATEGIES 14.2

■ **READING THE SECTION** As you read the section, match each of the following people or terms with the correct description by writing the letter of the description in the space provided.

_____ **1.** Willa Cather

_____ **2.** sod

_____ **3.** bonanza farms

_____ **4.** U.S. Department of Agriculture

_____ **5.** Exodusters

_____ **6.** Great Plains

_____ **7.** Morrill Act

_____ **8.** Homestead Act

_____ **9.** Pacific Railway Act

_____ **10.** Benjamin Singleton

a. gave 160 acres of land to people if they would farm it for five years

b. gave lands to railroad companies to build a railroad line linking the East and West Coasts

c. gave more than 17 million acres of federal land to the states

d. African American settlers who moved West to escape persecution in the South

e. former slave who led many African American settlers west

f. difficult environment for farming

g. helped farmers adapt to the new environment

h. material used for houses because wood was scarce

i. owned by large corporations and run like factories

j. famous writer who specialized in stories about midwestern American life

■ **POST-READING QUICK CHECK** After you have finished reading the section, write a brief summary of some of the reasons people wanted to move west and some of the hardships they faced once they got there.

_____

_____

_____

_____

_____

_____

_____

The Western Crossroads

GUIDED READING STRATEGIES 14.3

◼ **READING THE SECTION** As you read the section, list three significant points about each of the topics given.

Texas longhorn cattle

1. _____

2. _____

3. _____

Sheep ranching

1. _____

2. _____

3. _____

Towns and ranches

1. _____

2. _____

3. _____

◼ **POST-READING QUICK CHECK** After you have finished reading the section, write a brief summary of the reasons the cattle boom ended.

_____

_____

_____

Guided Reading Strategies

CHAPTER 14
The Western Crossroads

GUIDED READING STRATEGIES 14.4

■ READING THE SECTION As you read the section, examine each pair of statements below. Circle the letter of the statement in each pair that is true.

1. **a.** The Mother Lode was one of the world's richest gold veins.
   b. The Comstock Lode was one of the world's richest silver veins.

2. **a.** High-pressure water was used to blast away rock to expose minerals in a process known as strip mining.
   b. High-pressure water was used to blast away rock to expose minerals in a process known as hydraulic mining.

3. **a.** The United States's purchase of Alaska was referred to as "Seward's Folly."
   b. The United States's purchase of Eureka was referred to as "Seward's Folly."

4. **a.** Hard-rock mining used acid to extract gold from ore.
   b. The patio process used mercury to extract silver from ore.

5. **a.** Unions worked hard to abolish mining because of its dangers.
   b. Unions tried to improve the working conditions and wages of miners.

6. **a.** Elizabeth Collins was called the Cattle Queen of Montana.
   b. Elizabeth Collins was called the Mining Queen of Montana.

7. **a.** Hard-rock mining used the gradual scraping of the earth's surface to detect metals and minerals.
   b. Deep shafts were sunk into the earth in the process called hard-rock mining.

8. **a.** The Alaskan gold rush started when gold was discovered in Seward, Alaska.
   b. The Alaskan gold rush started when gold was discovered in the Yukon territory.

■ POST-READING QUICK CHECK After you have finished reading the section, in the space provided, list three changes that took place in mining camps as families began to join the settlers.

1. _____

2. _____

3. _____

CHAPTER 15

The Second Industrial Revolution

GUIDED READING STRATEGIES 15.1

■ **READING THE SECTION** As you read the section, use the graphic organizers to list three significant effects of changes in the following industries during the Second Industrial Revolution.

Steel
_____
_____
_____

Oil
_____
_____
_____

Transportation
_____
_____
_____

Communications
_____
_____
_____

■ **POST-READING QUICK CHECK** After you have finished reading the section, briefly explain the contributions each of the following people made to the Second Industrial Revolution.

1. Henry Bessemer: _____

2. Elijah McCoy: _____

3. Samuel F. B. Morse: _____

CHAPTER 15

The Second Industrial Revolution

GUIDED READING STRATEGIES 15.2

■ READING THE SECTION As you read the section, complete the missing information about the following terms or people.

1. Term: laissez-faire capitalism

Key point: _____

_____

2. Term: _____

Key point: Any attempts to help the poor slows social progress.

3. Term: corporation

Key point: _____

_____

4. Term: Gospel of Wealth

Key point: _____

_____

5. Person: Andrew Carnegie

Key point: _____

_____

6. Person: _____

Key point: one of the founders of the Standard Oil Company who was known for his tough business practices

7. Person: Cornelius Vanderbilt

Key point: _____

_____

8. Term: trust

Key point: _____

_____

9. Term: department stores

Key point: _____

_____

10. Term: _____

Key point: describes a situation where a trust gains complete control of an industry

■ POST-READING QUICK CHECK After you have finished reading the section, briefly explain the significance of each of the following people.

1. Karl Marx: _____

2. George Westinghouse: _____

3. George M. Pullman: _____

The Second Industrial Revolution

GUIDED READING STRATEGIES 15.3

█ READING THE SECTION As you read the section, match each of the following terms with the correct description by writing the letter of the description in the space provided.

_____ **1.** immigrants

_____ **2.** anarchists

_____ **3.** Sherman Antitrust Act

_____ **4.** Haymarket Riot

_____ **5.** Great Upheaval

_____ **6.** African Americans

_____ **7.** working conditions

_____ **8.** Pullman

_____ **9.** Samuel L. Gompers

_____ **10.** Mary Harris Jones

a. made monopolies and trusts illegal

b. people who were prevented from holding factory jobs in the south

c. group of people who entered the workforce in response to the demand for labor

d. characterized by long hours and low wages

e. active female union organizer for the Knights of Labor

f. a period of time when there were many strikes and violent confrontations between union members and police

g. people who were against all types of government

h. violent confrontation in Chicago stemming from the strike against the McCormick Harvesting Machine Company

i. created the American Federation of Labor (AFL)

j. strike that resulted at a sleeping-car factory when workers' wages were cut but prices at the company store were not

█ POST-READING QUICK CHECK After you have finished reading the section, identify the types of workers each of the following unions tried to enlist in their organizations.

1. Knights of Labor: _____

2. American Federation of Labor: _____

3. American Railway Union: _____

Guided Reading Strategies

The Transformation of American Society

GUIDED READING STRATEGIES 16.1

■ READING THE SECTION As you read the section, match each of the following terms with the correct description by writing the letter of the description in the space provided.

_____ **1.** steerage

_____ **2.** benevolent societies

_____ **3.** Chinese Exclusion Act

_____ **4.** Immigration Restriction League

_____ **5.** Ellis Island

_____ **6.** Angel Island

_____ **7.** nativists

_____ **8.** new immigrants

a. people who came to the United States from southern or eastern Europe

b. cheapest but also poorest accommodations on a ship crossing the ocean

c. opened in 1892 to receive European immigrants

d. located in San Francisco Bay, where Asian immigrants were received

e. charitable organizations formed to help immigrants

f. opposed immigration because they believed that immigrants took jobs from native-born Americans

g. law that denied citizenship to Chinese Americans and prohibited Chinese laborers from immigrating to the United States

h. group that wanted to impose a literacy test on all immigrants

■ POST-READING QUICK CHECK After you have finished reading the section, answer the following questions.

1. Were most of the immigrants well-educated, skilled workers?

_____

2. Why do you think an immigrant would suffer a difficult journey to come to the United States in the late 1890s?

_____

3. How did immigrants and their children react to efforts to Americanize them?

_____

The Transformation of American Society

CHAPTER 16

GUIDED READING STRATEGIES 16.2

■ **READING THE SECTION** As you read the section, supply the missing information about each of the following terms or people.

1. Person: Elisha Otis

Key point: _____

_____

2. Term: _____

Key point: forms of public transportation on which many people travel at one time

3. Term: suburbs

Key point: _____

_____

4. Term: nouveau riche

Key point: _____

_____

5. Term: conspicuous consumption

Key point: _____

_____

6. Term: _____

Key point: community centers staffed by volunteers and offering various services to the working class and poor

7. Person: Jane Addams

Key point: _____

_____

8. Person: _____

Key point: founded Locust Street Social Settlement, an African American settlement house

9. Term: Social Gospel

Key point: _____

_____

10. Person: Caroline Bartlett

Key point: _____

_____

■ **POST-READING QUICK CHECK** After you have finished reading the section, briefly compare middle-class life with working-class life in the following areas.

1. Education: _____

2. Types of jobs for women: _____

3. Living conditions: _____

Guided Reading Strategies

CHAPTER 16

The Transformation of American Society

GUIDED READING STRATEGIES 16.3

■ **READING THE SECTION** As you read the section, examine the riddles below. Solve each riddle by writing the correct name or term in the space provided.

_____ 1. "My 'Laboratory School' at the University of Chicago stressed cooperative 'learning by doing.'"

_____ 2. "I'm the sensationalistic news reporting that sold a lot of newspapers."

_____ 3. "As my popularity grew, I came to be called the 'national game of the United States.'"

_____ 4. "They called me the King of Ragtime for all the great songs I wrote."

_____ 5. "If you liked short skits, humor, and animal acts, you'd visit me."

_____ 6. "I was one of the few sports that encouraged both men and women to play."

_____ 7. "I required parents to send their kids to school."

_____ 8. "Despite the fact that 18 college students and 46 high school students died playing me, I continued to rise in popularity in the United States in the early 1900s."

_____ 9. "I stressed the importance of building lovely parks and public places to inspire patriotism in Americans."

_____ 10. "More and more literate Americans turned to me as a form of entertainment and leisure."

■ **POST-READING QUICK CHECK** After you have finished reading the section, in the space provided, briefly explain the roots of ragtime music and name two dances that became popular because of it.

_____

_____

_____

_____

Name _____ Class _____ Date _____

Politics in the Gilded Age

GUIDED READING STRATEGIES 17.1

■ **READING THE SECTION** As you read the section, complete the following chart by listing three benefits and three failings of political machines.

Political Machines

Benefits	Failings
_____	_____
_____	_____
_____	_____

■ **POST-READING QUICK CHECK** After you have finished reading the section, briefly explain how each of the following people is significant to the events described in Section 1.

1. Jim Pendergast   Significance: _____

_____

2. William Marcy Tweed   Significance: _____

_____

3. Thomas Nast   Significance: _____

_____

Politics in the Gilded Age

GUIDED READING STRATEGIES 17.2

■ **READING THE SECTION** As you read the section, supply the missing information about each of the following terms or people.

1. Term: Whiskey Ring

Key point: _____

_____

2. Term: _____

Key point: Practice of awarding civil service jobs based on patronage instead of merit

3. Term: Gilded Age

Key point: _____

_____

4. Term: Stalwarts

Key point: _____

_____

5. Term: _____

Key point: committed to political reform

6. Term: _____

Key point: assassinated four months after taking office, which allowed Chester A. Arthur to become president

7. Term: Pendleton Civil Service Act

Key point: _____

_____

8. Term: _____

Key point: Algonquian term for "big chiefs" used to describe Republicans supporting reform

9. Person: _____

Key point: committed to political reform, he increased the number of federal civil service jobs that required taking a test

10. Person: Benjamin Harrison

Key point: _____

_____

■ **POST-READING QUICK CHECK** After you have read the section briefly, explain some of the actions taken by President Harrison to overturn reforms instituted by Grover Cleveland.

_____

_____

_____

CHAPTER 17 — Politics in the Gilded Age

GUIDED READING STRATEGIES 17.3

■ READING THE SECTION As you read the section, match each of the following terms with the correct description by writing the letter of the description in the space provided.

_____ **1.** cooperatives

_____ **2.** Populist Party

_____ **3.** Interstate Commerce Act

_____ **4.** Cross of Gold

_____ **5.** Bland-Allison Act

_____ **6.** National Grange

_____ **7.** Colored Farmers' Alliance

_____ **8.** graduated income tax

_____ **9.** greenbacks

_____ **10.** gold standard

a. first major farmers' organization to address political and economic issues

b. an organization in which people pool their resources to buy and sell goods

c. tried to make sure that railroads charged fair prices for their shipping services

d. a proposal that suggested a person with a higher income should pay higher taxes

e. formed because the existing union would not allow African American farmers to become members

f. financial system based on the idea that a dollar was equal to a specific amount of gold

g. legislation that required the government to buy silver every month

h. new political party formed to advance the interests of farmers, laborers, and reformers

i. paper money used during the Civil War

j. a famous speech made by presidential candidate William Jennings Bryan that stressed the importance of using silver instead of gold as our monetary standard

■ POST-READING QUICK CHECK After you have finished reading the section, briefly explain the significance of the following people to the farmers' attempts to use political action to achieve their demands.

1. Mary Elizabeth Lease   Significance: _____

_____

2. James B. Weaver   Significance: _____

_____

CHAPTER 18 The Age of Reform

GUIDED READING STRATEGIES 18.1

■■ **READING THE SECTION** As you read the section, use the graphic organizer to list several important points about the Progressives and their effect on their society.

Progressives
Main Focus or Goal: _____
Key Person: _____
Key Issues: 1. _____
_____
2. _____
_____
3. _____
_____
Actions Taken: 1. _____
_____
2. _____
_____
3. _____
_____
4. _____
_____

■■ **POST-READING QUICK CHECK** After you have read the section, briefly answer the following questions.

1. Who were the muckrakers? _____

2. What did the muckrakers do to help or hinder the Progressive movement?

_____

The Age of Reform

CHAPTER 18

GUIDED READING STRATEGIES 18.2

■ **READING THE SECTION** As you read the section, state what you think this section's main idea is. Then use the graphic organizer to list two key points for each of the following topics.

The main idea: _____

_____

Labor Conditions	Triangle Shirtwaist Fire	*Muller* v. *Oregon*
1. _____	1. _____	1. _____
2. _____	2. _____	2. _____
AFL	**ILGW**	**IWW**
1. _____	1. _____	1. _____
2. _____	2. _____	2. _____

■ **POST-READING QUICK CHECK** After you have read the section, briefly explain why the following people were important to the issues discussed in this section.

1. Florence Kelley   Significance: _____

2. William "Big Bill" Haywood   Significance: _____

CHAPTER 18 The Age of Reform

GUIDED READING STRATEGIES 18.3

■ READING THE SECTION As you read the section, supply the missing information about each of the following terms or people.

1. Person: Lawrence Veiller

Key point: _____

_____

2. Term: _____

Key point: law that required tenements be built with health and sanitation features

3. Term: _____

Key point: involves developing parks, building codes, and sanitation standards and zoning

4. Term: prohibition

Key point: _____

_____

5. Term: _____

Key point: started out as an organization that crusaded against alcohol but became a national force on other issues including women's rights

6. Term: Eighteenth Amendment

Key point: _____

_____

7. Term: _____

Key point: inexpensive and popular new form of entertainment, especially for the urban poor

8. Person: W. E. B. Du Bois

Key point: _____

_____

9. Term: NAACP

Key point: _____

_____

10. Term: _____

Key point: tried to improve job opportunities and housing for African Americans, especially for migrants moving north from the southern states; worked closely with NAACP to achieve its goals

11. Term: _____

Key point: formed to address problems faced by American Indians including civil rights, health, and education

12. Term: assimilation

Key point: _____

_____

■ POST-READING QUICK CHECK After you have read the section, briefly explain the reasons some progressives also favored immigration restrictions.

_____

_____

Progressive Politicians

CHAPTER
19

GUIDED READING STRATEGIES 19.1

■ **READING THE SECTION** As you read the section, use each clue below to write the term or name in the space provided. Then unscramble the boxed letters to identify the focus of Section 1.

1. Election reform measure that forces the legislature to place a recently passed law on the ballot:

   __ __ ▢ __ __ __ __ __ __ __ __ __

2. Amendment that gave voters the power to elect their senators directly:

   __ ▢ __ __ __ __ __ __ __ __ __ __ __ __ __ ▢ __ __ __ __ __ ▢ __

3. List of candidates on a single, uniform sheet of paper:

   __ __ __ __ ▢ __ __ __ __ __ __ ▢ __ __

4. Election reform measure that enables voters to call for a special election to remove an elected official from office:

   ▢ __ __ __ __ __ __

5. Nominating election in which voters choose the candidates who later run in a general election:

   __ __ ▢ __ __ __ __ __ __ __ ▢ __ __ __ __

6. Election reform measure that gives voters the power to introduce legislation:

   __ __ __ __ __ __ __ __ __ ▢ __ __

7. Form of city government run by experts in their fields rather than by party loyalists:

   __ __ ▢ __ __ __ __ __ __ __ __ __ __ ▢ __

8. Expert administrator hired to run a city like a business:

   __ __ __ ▢ __ __ __ __ ▢ __ __ __

9. Model state reform program: __ __ __ __ __ __ __ __ ▢ __ __ __ __ __

10. Wisconsin governor in 1900 known for his state reform policies:

    __ __ __ __ ▢ __ __ __ __ __ __ __ __ __ __ __ __ __ ▢ __

Focus of Section 1: ▢▢▢▢▢▢▢▢▢▢ ▢▢▢▢▢▢

■ **POST-READING QUICK CHECK** After you have finished reading the section, in the space provided, name two important reform mayors from this time period and the city that each governed.

CHAPTER 19 Progressive Politicians

GUIDED READING STRATEGIES 19.2

■ **READING THE SECTION** As you read the section, complete the graphic organizer by supplying one or two examples of each of the ways that the Roosevelt administration attempted to regulate business.

Trust-busting

1. _____

2. _____

Railroad Regulation

1. _____

2. _____

Roosevelt Regulates Business

Meat Industry Regulation

1. _____

Food and Drug Industry Regulation

1. _____

■ **POST-READING QUICK CHECK** After you have finished reading the section, in the space provided, tell how the term *Square Deal* came about and explain its meaning.

_____

_____

_____

_____

_____

Progressive Politicians

CHAPTER 19

GUIDED READING STRATEGIES 19.3

■ **READING THE SECTION** As you read the section, examine the riddles below. Solve each riddle by writing the correct name or term in the space provided.

_____ 1. "President Roosevelt supported me because he felt I had the same reform tendencies that he did."

_____ 2. "I extended the regulatory power of the Interstate Commerce Commission to telephone and telegraph companies."

_____ 3. "Progressives were happy to see me ratified in 1913, because they considered me a fair way to fund government programs."

_____ 4. "President Taft took a lot of heat for signing me, which changed the tariff rates."

_____ 5. "I am the conflict that arose when President Taft fired his head of the U.S. Forest Service."

_____ 6. "I am the tobacco-chewing Speaker of the House who made waves by preventing bills from reaching the House floor for debate."

_____ 7. "I was also called the Bull Moose Party and was headed by Theodore Roosevelt."

_____ 8. "I was full of proposals to help small businesses."

_____ 9. "I was the Socialist Party candidate for president in 1912."

_____ 10. "I am the former Princeton University professor who became president in 1912."

■ **POST-READING QUICK CHECK** After you have finished reading the section, in the space provided, state the four key points of Woodrow Wilson's New Freedom platform from the presidential election of 1912.

1. _____

2. _____

3. _____

4. _____

Guided Reading Strategies

CHAPTER 19 Progressive Politicians

GUIDED READING STRATEGIES 19.4

▮▮ **READING THE SECTION** As you read the section, complete the graphic organizer by supplying examples of legislation enacted by the Wilson administration.

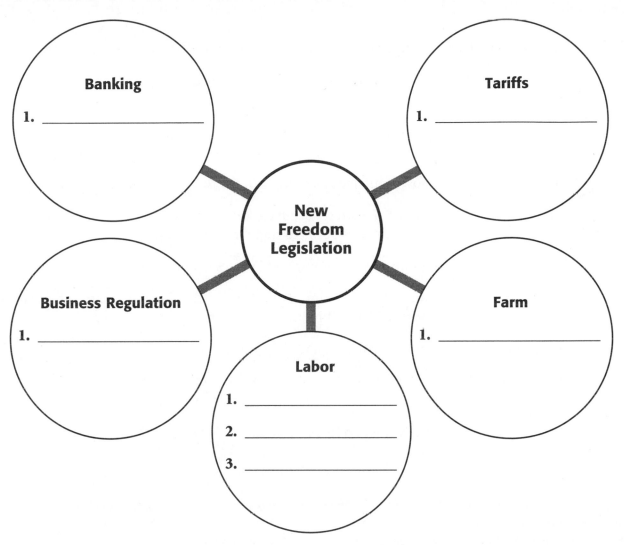

Banking

1. _____

Tariffs

1. _____

New Freedom Legislation

Business Regulation

1. _____

Farm

1. _____

Labor

1. _____

2. _____

3. _____

▮▮ **POST-READING QUICK CHECK** After you have finished reading the section, in the space provided, list two women who were significant to the struggle for women's suffrage and summarize their approaches.

1. Person: _____   Approach: _____

_____

2. Person: _____   Approach: _____

_____

America and the World

GUIDED READING STRATEGIES 20.1

■ **READING THE SECTION** Review the list of events before reading the section. Then as you read the section, number the following events in the order in which they occurred.

_____ **1.** President Theodore Roosevelt negotiates a peace treaty between Japan and Russia.

_____ **2.** Japan rapidly transforms itself into an industrial power and builds up its army and navy.

_____ **3.** Japan defeats China, seizing China's Liaotung Peninsula, the large island of Taiwan, and Korea.

_____ **4.** Japan exists in almost complete isolation from the rest of the world.

_____ **5.** Commodore Matthew Perry presents gifts to the Japanese rulers and tries to persuade them to open Japan's doors to trade with the West.

_____ **6.** Japan emerges as an imperialist power and invades China.

_____ **7.** Commodore Matthew Perry sails into Edo, (present-day Tokyo) Japan, with seven warships on President Millard Fillmore's instructions.

_____ **8.** The Japanese leaders agree to Western demands for trade.

_____ **9.** President Roosevelt sends the "Great White Fleet" to the Japanese port of Yokohama as a reminder of the United States' military might.

_____ **10.** Japanese troops attack Russian forces in Manchuria, starting the Russo-Japanese War.

■ **POST-READING QUICK CHECK** After you have finished reading the section, in the space provided, state the three principles of the Open Door Policy that would allow all nations equal access to trade and investment in China.

1. Principle: _____

_____

2. Principle: _____

_____

3. Principle: _____

_____

CHAPTER 20

America and the World

GUIDED READING STRATEGIES 20.2

■ **READING THE SECTION** As you read the section, complete the following chart by listing four reasons for the annexation of the Philippines and one reason against the annexation.

Debate over the Annexation of the Philippines

For Annexation	Against Annexation
1. _____	1. _____
2. _____	
3. _____	
4. _____	

■ **POST-READING QUICK CHECK** After you have finished reading the section, in the space provided, list the four terms of the peace treaty agreed to by Spain at the end of the Spanish-American War.

1. _____

2. _____

3. _____

4. _____

CHAPTER 20

America and the World

GUIDED READING STRATEGIES 20.3

■ READING THE SECTION As you read the section, match each of the following terms with the correct description by writing the letter of the description in the space provided.

_____ 1. Hay–Bunau-Varilla Treaty

_____ 2. Platt Amendment

_____ 3. dollar diplomacy

_____ 4. yellow fever

_____ 5. Jones Act of 1917

_____ 6. protectorate

_____ 7. Roosevelt Corollary

_____ 8. Monroe Doctrine

_____ 9. Foraker Act

_____ 10. high-interest bank loans

a. legislation that limited Cuba's freedom to make treaties with countries other than the United States and authorized the United States to intervene in Cuban affairs as it saw necessary

b. relationship between two countries in which one promises to protect the other from other nations but also reserves the right to intervene in the protected country's affairs

c. legislation that provided that Puerto Rico's governor and upper house of legislature be appointed by the United States and that the lower house be elected by Puerto Ricans

d. granted Puerto Ricans U.S. citizenship and allowed them the right to elect both houses of their legislature

e. legislation that gave the United States complete and unending sovereignty over a 10-mile-wide Canal Zone in the Republic of Panama

f. tropical disease spread by mosquitoes

g. doctrine that was established in 1823 but rarely used until after the Spanish-American War

h. pledge stating that the United States would use force against any European nation attempting to seize Dominican territory

i. President Taft's policy of using American economic influence as a means of protecting U.S. interests in Latin America

j. hard-to-repay loans offered to many Latin American countries

■ POST-READING QUICK CHECK After you have finished reading the section, in the space provided, name three people involved with the treaty for the Panama Canal and state their significance.

1. Person: _____ Significance: _____

2. Person: _____ Significance: _____

3. Person: _____ Significance: _____

America and the World

GUIDED READING STRATEGIES 20.4

■ **READING THE SECTION** As you read the section, examine the riddles below. Solve each riddle by writing the correct name or term in the space provided.

_____ 1. "I am the Mexican president who won an amazing eight terms in office."

_____ 2. "I am a former tenant farmer who became a rebel against Díaz."

_____ 3. "My book encouraged many intellectuals to stage a revolution."

_____ 4. "I succeeded Díaz as leader of Mexico and my government was recognized by the United States."

_____ 5. "I am a commanding general who eventually became the head of Mexico but was disliked by Woodrow Wilson."

_____ 6. "I took over Mexico promising to protect Americans, and this led to my acceptance by the United States."

_____ 7. "I am the general who defeated Villa's troops."

_____ 8. "I am the Mexican revolutionary who raided the town of Columbus, new Mexico, out of anger at the United States."

_____ 9. "I am an American general who pursued a Mexican rebel deep into Mexico but never caught him."

_____ 10. "When it came to Pancho Villa, I wanted him dead or alive."

■ **POST-READING QUICK CHECK** After you have finished reading the section, In the space provided, state five revolutionary ideas contained in the new Mexican constitution developed by the Carranza government and put into effect in 1917.

1. _____

2. _____

3. _____

4. _____

5. _____

CHAPTER 21

World War I

GUIDED READING STRATEGIES 21.1

■ **READING THE SECTION** As you read the section, in the space provided, complete the flowchart summarizing the events that took place in June 1914 that began the Great War.

> Austro-Hungarian _____ visits Sarajevo, Bosnia

⬇

> _____ nationalist _____
> shoots and kills the archduke and his wife

⬇

> _____ declares war on Serbia

⬇

> Local conflict turns into a global war

⬇   ⬇

> Germany offers its support to
>
> _____

> Russia offers its support to
>
> _____

⬇   ⬇

> The _____ and
> Bulgaria join with Austria-Hungary to
>
> form the _____ Powers

> Britain and _____
> join with Serbia to form the
>
> _____ Powers

■ **POST-READING QUICK CHECK** After you have finished reading the section, in the space provided, list three new weapons that were first used in the Great War.

1. _____

2. _____

3. _____

CHAPTER
21
World War I

GUIDED READING STRATEGIES 21.2

■ **READING THE SECTION** Each of the following sentences contains an underlined word, phrase, or name that makes the sentence incorrect. As you read the section, use the space provided to write the word, phrase, or name that makes the sentence correct.

_____ **1.** The policy of staying out of a conflict is called <u>Non-Meddling</u>

_____ **2.** The United States grew angry with Germany after they sank the <u>Sussex</u>, killing 128 Americans.

_____ **3.** Secretary of State <u>William Baruch</u> resigned in anger after President Wilson issued ultimatums to Germany.

_____ **4.** The <u>Peace</u> Pledge was a promise by Germany not to sink ocean liners without warning them first.

_____ **5.** President Wilson passed the <u>Preparedness Act</u> to prepare American soldiers for the possibility of war.

_____ **6.** In the <u>Schwartzstein Note</u>, Germany asked Mexico to enter a military alliance against the United States.

_____ **7.** Congress passed the <u>War Powers Act</u> to draft men aged 21–30 into the armed forces.

_____ **8.** Both <u>whites</u> and African Americans faced harsh discrimination in the army during the war.

_____ **9.** General <u>James G. Smith</u> was the leader of the American troops in France in 1917.

_____ **10.** The <u>group</u> system was used to safely ferry American merchant vessels across the Atlantic Ocean.

■ **POST-READING QUICK CHECK** After you have finished reading the section, in the space provided, list five groups of Americans that favored the Central Powers at the beginning of the war.

1. _____

2. _____

3. _____

4. _____

5. _____

CHAPTER 21 World War I

GUIDED READING STRATEGIES 21.3

■ **READING THE SECTION** As you read the section, complete the following chart by supplying the missing information about each of the following federal war boards discussed in Section 3.

Federal War Boards

Name of Board	Administrator(s)	Purpose
Food Administration	_____	_____ _____ _____
_____	_____	regulated the production and supply of fuel
_____	William McAdoo	_____ _____ _____
_____	_____	had overall responsibility for allocating scarce materials, establishing production priorities, and setting prices

■ **POST-READING QUICK CHECK** After you have finished reading the section, in the space provided, discuss the importance of women to the war effort at home and its effect on women's suffrage.

_____

_____

_____

_____

_____

_____

CHAPTER 21 World War I

GUIDED READING STRATEGIES 21.4

■ **READING THE SECTION** Review the list of events before reading the section. Then as you read the section, number the events in the order in which they occurred.

_____ 1. The Germans are halted and Paris is saved.

_____ 2. General Pershing allows U.S. troops to be placed under the command of Marshal Ferdinand Foch of France.

_____ 3. French and American Allied troops led by Foch push the Germans back at Reims, turning the tide in favor of the Allies.

_____ 4. A division of U.S. Marines recaptures Belleau Woods and two other towns.

_____ 5. The Germans perform a final assault near Reims, but the Allied lines hold.

_____ 6. U.S. troops help the French stop the Germans at Château-Thierry.

_____ 7. The Allied offensive fails, and the morale of the Allied troops is shattered.

_____ 8. The Germans launch a tremendous offensive, some 1 million soldiers strong, against the Allies and come within 50 miles of Paris.

_____ 9. The United States joins the Allied forces, and an Allied offensive is launched to break the deadlock on the Western front.

_____ 10. Russia withdraws from the war after the czar is overthrown by the Bolsheviks led by Vladimir Lenin.

■ **POST-READING QUICK CHECK** After you have finished reading the section, in the space provided, list the members of the Big Four and their countries.

1. _____

2. _____

3. _____

4. _____

A Turbulent Decade

CHAPTER 22

GUIDED READING STRATEGIES 22.1

■ **READING THE SECTION** As you read the section, complete the following chart by supplying the missing information about each of the strikes of 1919 discussed in Section 1.

The Strikes of 1919

Name of Strike	Date	Demands	Outcome
Seattle general strike (shipyard workers)	_____	_____	no violence; ended in 5 days with no demands met
_____	September 1919	better pay and working conditions	_____
Steel strike of 1919	_____	_____	strikers jailed, beaten, or shot; strike called off January 9, 1920
_____	November 1919	discontinuance of wartime contract keeping workers' pay at 1917 rates, shorter hours	_____

■ **POST-READING QUICK CHECK** After you have finished reading the section, in the space provided, compare and contrast the Marxist-inspired Socialist Party of Eugene Debs with the revolutionary Marxism of the Communists.

_____

_____

_____

_____

_____

A Turbulent Decade

GUIDED READING STRATEGIES 22.2

■ **READING THE SECTION** As you read the section, complete the graphic organizers by supplying the missing information about each of the presidential elections.

Presidential Election of 1920

Party/presidential candidate:

1. Won: _____   **2.** Lost: _____

Significance: _____

_____

_____

Presidential Election of 1924

Party/presidential candidate:

1. Won: _____   **2.** Lost: _____

3. Lost: _____

Significance: _____

_____

Presidential Election of 1928

Party/presidential candidate:

1. Won: _____   **2.** Lost: _____

Significance: _____

_____

_____

■ **POST-READING QUICK CHECK** After you have finished reading the section, in the space provided, state the two main economic goals of the Harding administration.

1. Goal: _____

2. Goal: _____

A Turbulent Decade

CHAPTER 22

GUIDED READING STRATEGIES 22.3

■ **READING THE SECTION** As you read the section, complete the following out-line by supplying the main idea and the missing subtopics and supporting details.

A Nation Divided

Main Idea: _____

_____

Topic I: _____

      Detail A: They move for economic opportunities and freedom from discrimination.

      Detail B: _____

Topic II: The Ku Klux Klan is reborn.

Topic III: _____

      Detail A: _____

      Detail B: African Americans work to eliminate discrimination in the workplace.

      Detail C: _____

Topic IV: _____

Topic V: Mexican immigrants not affected by the restrictive legislation.

Topic VI: _____

■ **POST-READING QUICK CHECK** After you have finished reading the section, in the space provided, state the three key points of the Immigration Act of 1924.

1. _____

_____

2. _____

_____

3. _____

_____

CHAPTER 23 The Jazz Age

GUIDED READING STRATEGIES 23.1

■ **READING THE SECTION** As you read the section, complete the graphic organizer by supplying two examples of ways that the automobile changed American life.

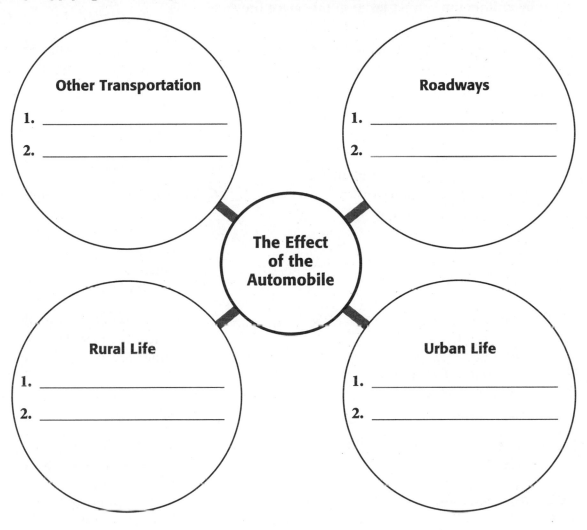

Other Transportation

1. _____
2. _____

Roadways

1. _____
2. _____

The Effect of the Automobile

Rural Life

1. _____
2. _____

Urban Life

1. _____
2. _____

■ **POST-READING QUICK CHECK** After you have finished reading the section, in the space provided, state the three main reasons for soaring economic growth in the 1920s.

1. _____

2. _____

3. _____

The Jazz Age

GUIDED READING STRATEGIES 23.2

■ **READING THE SECTION** Read through the following sentences. Then, as you read the section, match each of the descriptions with the name of the person being described by writing the correct letter in the space provided.

_____ **1.** A powerful gangster of the 1920s was
a. Eliot Ness.
b. Al Capone.
c. Clarence Darrow.
d. Cecil B. DeMille.

_____ **2.** The special agent who put an end to Al Capone's reign over the Chicago underworld was
a. Eliot Ness.
b. Billy Sunday.
c. Cecil B. DeMille.
d. Jim Thorpe.

_____ **3.** The movie director famous for his epic plots was
a. Charlie Chaplin.
b. Cecil B. DeMille.
c. Lon Chaney.
d. Al Jolson.

_____ **4.** The leader of the "Black Sox" scandal of 1919 was
a. Jim Thorpe.
b. Babe Ruth.
c. Joe Jackson.
d. Ty Cobb.

_____ **5.** The first athlete to win both the pentathlon and the decathlon at the Olympics was
a. Jim Thorpe.
b. Babe Ruth.
c. Eliot Ness.
d. Red Grange.

_____ **6.** The first person to fly nonstop between New York and Paris was
a. Charles Darwin.
b. Tom Mix.
c. Amelia Earhart.
d. Charles Lindbergh.

_____ **7.** The first woman to cross the Atlantic Ocean by plane was
a. Aimee Semple McPherson.
b. Greta Garbo.
c. Amelia Earhart.
d. Babe Ruth.

_____ **8.** A glitzy Christian revivalist was
a. Aimee Semple McPherson.
b. Billy Sunday.
c. Charles Lindbergh.
d. Charlie Chaplin.

■ **POST-READING QUICK CHECK** After you have finished reading the section, in the space provided, tell what each of the following prohibition laws did.

1. Eighteenth Amendment: _____

_____

2. Volstead Act: _____

3. Twenty-first Amendment: _____

CHAPTER 23 · The Jazz Age

GUIDED READING STRATEGIES 23.3

■ READING THE SECTION As you read the section, complete the chart by placing each of the following names in the proper column.

Alfred Steiglitz	Langston Hughes	Frank Lloyd Wright	Bessie Smith
Louis Armstrong	Rose McClendon	F. Scott Fitzgerald	Diego Rivera
Edward Hopper	Paul Robeson	James Weldon Johnson	Duke Ellington
Bix Biederbecke	Sinclair Lewis	George Gershwin	Ernest Hemingway

Creative Arts in the 1920s

Music	Theater	Literature	Visual Arts
_____	_____	_____	_____
_____	_____	_____	_____
_____		_____	_____
_____		_____	_____
_____		_____	

■ POST-READING QUICK CHECK After you have finished reading the section, in the space provided, explain how blues and jazz sprang from African American culture.

_____

_____

_____

_____

_____

_____

_____

_____

_____

The Great Depression

GUIDED READING STRATEGIES 24.1

■ **READING THE SECTION** As you read the section, think about the things that led up to the depression, then complete the following outline by supplying the missing supporting details.

Hard Times

I. Purchasing with Credit

  Detail A: _____

  Detail B: _____

  Detail C: _____

II: Playing the Market

  Detail A: _____

  Detail B: Too much stock speculation.

  Detail C: _____

III: Bull Market vs. Bear Market

  Detail A: _____

  Detail B: _____

  Detail C: _____

IV: Black Thursday

  Detail A: _____

  Detail B: Prices plunged.

  Detail C: _____

V: Black Tuesday

  Detail A: Prices sunk to lowest value.

  Detail B: _____

  Detail C: _____

VI: Banking Crisis

  Detail A: Borrowers couldn't pay loans.

  Detail B: _____

  Detail C: _____

VII: Business Failures

  Detail A: _____

  Detail B: _____

  Detail C: Huge unemployment

VIII: Global Depression

  Detail A: _____

  Detail B: World trade drops.

  Detail C: _____

IX: Income Gap

  Detail A: _____

  Detail B: _____

  Detail C: _____

■ **POST-READING QUICK CHECK** After you have finished reading the section, briefly explain how France kept unemployment low during the global depression.

_____

_____

Guided Reading Strategies

CHAPTER 24 The Great Depression

GUIDED READING STRATEGIES 24.2

■ READING THE SECTION As you read the section, match each of the following people or terms with the correct description by writing the letter of the description in the space provided.

_____ 1. breadlines

_____ 2. farms

_____ 3. *mutualistas*

_____ 4. James T. Farrell

_____ 5. Josefina Fierro de Bright

_____ 6. William Faulkner

_____ 7. apples

_____ 8. divorce

_____ 9. movies

_____ 10. shantytowns

a. items President Hoover believed people had quit their jobs to sell

b. mutual aid societies formed by Mexican Americans to help each other

c. lines formed by hungry people to get bowls of soup and bread

d. makeshift shelters built out of thrown-away items; also called "Hoovervilles"

e. rural businesses hit hard by the depression

f. Mexican American activist who led boycotts and marches to help Hispanic Americans during the depression

g. legal action whose numbers increased due to the severe economic hardship caused by the depression

h. a particularly popular method of escape for depression-era people

i. author who wrote about the hardships of Chicago's Irish immigrants

j. author who wrote many stories about small-town life in the South

■ POST-READING QUICK CHECK After you have finished reading the section, briefly describe the characteristics of a movie hero or heroine during the depression years.

_____

_____

_____

_____

_____

CHAPTER 24 The Great Depression

GUIDED READING STRATEGIES 24.3

■ **READING THE SECTION** As you read the section, list the key points for each heading.

1. Hoover's Philosophy	2. Boosting the Economy	3. Rumblings of Discontent
• _____ _____	• Departure from laissez-faire approach to government.	• _____ _____
• _____ _____	• _____ _____	• _____ _____
• Economic recovery would come through individual efforts.	• _____ _____	• _____ _____
• _____ _____	• _____ _____	• Farmers band together to stop farm foreclosures.
• _____ _____	• _____ _____	• _____ _____

■ **POST-READING QUICK CHECK** After you have finished reading the section, list three things about Franklin D. Roosevelt that made him an attractive candidate for positive change.

1. _____

2. _____

3. _____

The New Deal

CHAPTER 25

GUIDED READING STRATEGIES 25.1

■ **READING THE SECTION** As you read the section, complete the graphic organizers by supplying missing information about each person or term.

1. Term: _____ **Key Point:** A series of relief and recovery programs introduced by Franklin Delano Roosevelt to help the American people after the depression.	**3. Person:** _____ **Key Point:** Headed the FERA. Created the CWA, which helped unemployed people during the depression. Employed some 4 million people.	**5. Term:** _____ **Key Point:** Designed to help businesses and reduce unemployment. Created Public Works Administration and National Recovery Administration.	**7. Person:** _____ **Key Point:** African American economic scholar appointed as an adviser on racial matters to the Department of the Interior.
2. Term: Federal Deposit Insurance Corporation **Key Point:** _____ _____ _____ _____	**4. Term:** _____ **Key Point:** Created to help unemployed young men. Developed park trails, campgrounds, and beaches. Responsible for planting millions of trees.	**6. Term:** Tennessee Valley Authority (TVA) **Key Point:** _____ _____ _____ _____	**8. Person:** _____ **Key Point:** Founded the American Indian Defense Association. Appointed commissioner of Indian affairs. Worked to revitalize Indian life and culture.

■ **POST-READING QUICK CHECK** After you have finished reading the section, briefly explain Eleanor Roosevelt's reaction to the struggles African Americans faced in the late 1930s.

_____

_____

_____

_____

The New Deal

CHAPTER 25

GUIDED READING STRATEGIES 25.2

■ **READING THE SECTION** As you read the section, list two or three key points about each of the topics identified below.

1. Share-Our-Wealth

   • _____

   • _____

   • _____

2. Works Progress Administration

   • _____

   • _____

   • _____

3. National Youth Administration

   • _____

   • _____

   • _____

4. Mary McLeod Bethune

   • _____

   • _____

   • _____

5. Social Security Act

   • _____

   • _____

   • _____

6. Gas and Electricity

   • _____

   • _____

7. Wagner-Connery Act

   • _____

   • _____

   • _____

8. Congress of Industrial Organizations

   • _____

   • _____

   • _____

9. Farm Security Administration

   • _____

   • _____

■ **POST-READING QUICK CHECK** After you have finished reading the section, list two liberal reformers who were against the New Deal and explain what actions they wanted the government to take.

1. _____

   _____

   _____

2. _____

   _____

   _____

Guided Reading Strategies

CHAPTER 25 The New Deal

GUIDED READING STRATEGIES 25.3

■ **READING THE SECTION** As you read the section, match each of the following terms with the correct description by writing the letter of the description in the space provided.

_____ **1.** Dorothea Lange

_____ **2.** Okies

_____ **3.** electrification

_____ **4.** Gordon Parks

_____ **5.** Field Workers Union

_____ **6.** Woody Guthrie

_____ **7.** photography

_____ **8.** Dust Bowl

_____ **9.** Margaret Bourke-White

_____ **10.** *Migrant Mother*

a. 50 million-acre wasteland

b. term used to describe migrants coming to California from Oklahoma and other states

c. combined organization for Mexican American and Filipino workers

d. used to document the lives of ordinary Americans

e. African American photographer who became a filmmaker

f. international photojournalist

g. one of the most famous photographers, whose pictures reflected the sufferings of the homeless

h. well-known folk singer who sang about the experiences of common people

i. name of the photograph considered a masterpiece in its description of dignity as well as suffering

j. considered by a southern historian as "one of the most significant stimulants for modernization of the rural South"

■ **POST-READING QUICK CHECK** After you have finished reading the section, briefly describe what Mexican American, African American, and Filipino migrants all had in common during the depression.

_____

_____

_____

_____

_____

The New Deal

GUIDED READING STRATEGIES 25.4

■ **READING THE SECTION** As you read the section, identify the goals for each of the projects that were part of the overall Federal Project Number One, examples of works each produced, and two people who were prominent in those fields.

Federal Project Number One

Federal Writers' Project	Federal Theater Project	Federal Music Project	Federal Arts Project
Goal: _____ _____	Goal: _____ _____	Goal: create government-funded jobs for musicians.	Goal: _____ _____
Example of Works: state travel guides; oral histories of former slaves	Example of Works: _____	Example of Works: _____	Example of Works: _____
Prominent People: _____ _____	Prominent People: _____ Thornton Wilder	Prominent People: _____	Prominent People: Grant Wood

■ **POST-READING QUICK CHECK** After you have finished reading the section, choose two popular films from the era and describe the message you think viewers might have received.

1. _____

_____

_____

2. _____

_____

_____

CHAPTER 26

The Road to War

GUIDED READING STRATEGIES 26.1

■■ **READING THE SECTION** As you read the section, circle the boldface word or phrase that *best* completes each statement below.

1. The policy of withdrawing from world affairs is called **isolationism/hermitism**.

2. Reducing the size of military arsenals is referred to as **unloading/disarmament**.

3. The Washington Conference focused on reducing the size of the Allied nations' **air forces/navies**.

4. **Charles Evans Hughes/Warren G. Harding** was the leader of the Washington Conference.

5. The Kellogg-Briand Pact outlawed **nuclear weapons/war** as an instrument of national policy.

6. In September 1931, **Japan/Germany** attacked Manchuria, a section of China.

7. Germany considered the war reparations it was forced to pay as **fair/too harsh**.

8. Germany's war reparations **helped/hurt** its economy.

■■ **POST-READING QUICK CHECK** After you have finished reading the section, briefly explain why Americans wanted a policy of isolationism.

_____

_____

_____

_____

_____

_____

_____

CHAPTER 26

The Road to War

GUIDED READING STRATEGIES 26.2

READING THE SECTION As you read the section, match each of the following people or terms with the correct description by writing the letter of the description in the space provided.

_____ **1.** Lázaro Cárdenas

_____ **2.** United Fruit

_____ **3.** Josephus Daniels

_____ **4.** caudillos

_____ **5.** Augusto César Sandino

_____ **6.** Anastasio Somoza

_____ **7.** Emiliano Chamorro

_____ **8.** banana republic

_____ **9.** Good Neighbor policy

_____ **10.** Henry Stimson

a. overthrew the Nicaraguan government in 1925 and sparked a civil war

b. sent by President Coolidge to negotiate between opposing forces in Nicaragua

c. opposed American presence in Nicaragua and fought against them for many years

d. ordered the assassination of César Sandino, then took over the Nicaraguan presidency

e. intention of the United States to no longer intervene in the domestic activities of South American nations

f. term for a Latin American country that was run largely to serve the interests of foreign companies

g. largest American company in Latin America

h. nationalized Mexican oil industry when American companies refused to raise wages and improve working conditions

i. Roosevelt's ambassador to Mexico

j. military leaders who use force to maintain order

POST-READING QUICK CHECK After you have finished reading the section, briefly explain why American companies were able to create banana republics.

_____

_____

_____

_____

_____

Guided Reading Strategies

■ **READING THE SECTION** As you read the section, identify the major militaristic leaders and their governments. Then list three important points about them in terms of the information covered in the section.

Fascism

Italy	Soviet Union	Germany	Spain	Japan
Leader: _____ _____	Leader: _____ _____	Leader: _____ _____	Leader: _____ _____	Leader: _____ _____
Important Actions: • limited freedom of speech • _____ _____ • _____ _____	Important Actions: • _____ _____ • _____ _____ • created a totalitarian state	Important Actions: • claimed dictatorial powers • _____ _____ • _____ _____	Important Actions: • _____ _____ • initiated the Spanish Civil War • _____ _____	Important Actions: • _____ _____ • _____ _____ • bombed Chinese cities

■ **POST-READING QUICK CHECK** After you have finished reading the section, briefly explain the United States' reactions to the following events.

1. Italy's Invasion of Ethiopia   U.S. reaction: _____

2. *Kristallnacht*   U.S. reaction: _____

3. Spanish Civil War   U.S. reaction: _____

The Road to War

GUIDED READING STRATEGIES 26.4

■ **READING THE SECTION** As you read the section, examine each of the pairs of statements below. Circle the letter of the statement in each pair that is true.

1. **a.** Germany and Italy formed an alliance called the Axis Powers.
   b. The Allied Powers were a military alliance comprised of Italy, Germany, and France.

2. **a.** The leaders of the Munich Conference refused to grant Hitler the Sudetenland.
   b. The leaders of the Munich Conference granted Hitler the Sudetenland to appease him.

3. **a.** In late 1937, 54% of Americans believed the United States should withdraw from China to avoid the risk of war.
   b. By 1937 most Americans were eager to engage in war.

4. **a.** Stalin and Hitler signed a nonaggression pact that allowed each to attack the other if war broke out in Europe.
   b. Hitler and Stalin signed a nonaggression pact which stated they would not attack each other.

5. **a.** President Roosevelt took steps to help European nations that were being attacked.
   b. President Roosevelt insisted that the United States should not help any countries in the conflict in Europe.

6. **a.** Congress passed the Lend-Lease Act in 1941 to assist non-Allied countries fight the war.
   b. The Lend-Lease Act was passed to provide military supplied to non-Axis countries.

7. **a.** Roosevelt and Churchill created the Atlantic Charter, which called for freedom of international trade and the right for each nation to decide its own form of government.
   b. The Atlantic Charter was rejected by Stalin and Churchill on the grounds that it did not help developing nations.

8. **a.** In June 1941 the Soviet Union attacked Germany.
   b. In June 1941 Germany attacked the Soviet Union.

9. **a.** By 1941, the Japanese had begun to occupy land in Asia.
   b. The Japanese refused to attack other nations based on their religious beliefs.

10. **a.** On December 7, 1941, the United States attacked the Japanese fleet at Pearl Harbor, Hawaii.
    b. On December 7, 1941, the Japanese attacked the United States fleet at Pearl Harbor, Hawaii.

■ **POST-READING QUICK CHECK** After you have finished reading the section, briefly explain why some politicians thought appeasing Hitler was a good strategy.

_____

_____

_____

_____

Americans in World War II

GUIDED READING STRATEGIES 27.1

■ READING THE SECTION As you read the section, examine each of the pairs of statements below. Circle the letter of the statement in each pair that is true.

1. **a.** At the start of World War II, Germany and Japan had firm control over the areas they had invaded.
   b. At the start of World War II, Germany and Japan were struggling to control the areas they had invaded.

2. **a.** When the United States changed its factories over to wartime production, the economy faltered.
   b. When the United States changed its factories over to wartime production, the economy improved so much the Great Depression ended.

3. **a.** President Roosevelt created the War Production Board to increase military production.
   b. President Roosevelt created the War Production Board to boost the agricultural economy.

4. **a.** The Selective Service and Training Act made entering the war optional for young men aged 21 to 35.
   b. The Selective Service and Training Act required all young men aged 21 to 35 to register for the draft.

5. **a.** The Bataan Death March allowed the United States to subdue Japan in the Philippines.
   b. In the Bataan Death March, American and Filipino soldiers were treated harshly by the Japanese.

6. **a.** The United States won the Battle of Midway because it learned about the Japanese fleet's movements ahead of time.
   b. The United States won the Battle of Midway because the Japanese did not adequately prepare for the battle.

7. **a.** In the first half of 1942, German U-boats sunk more than 500 ships off the eastern coast of the United States.
   b. In the first half of 1942, German U-boats were completely stopped from sinking ships off the eastern coast of the United States.

8. **a.** The Battle of Stalingrad saw the Germans battle both the Soviet Union and the United States.
   b. The Battle of Stalingrad saw the Germans battle both the Soviet Union and the harsh Russian winter.

■ POST-READING QUICK CHECK After you have finished reading the section, briefly explain the effect of the Battle of Stalingrad on Germany's war efforts.

_____

_____

Americans in World War II

GUIDED READING STRATEGIES 27.2

■ READING THE SECTION As you read the section, match each of the following people or terms with the correct description by writing the letter of the description in the space provided.

_____ **1.** braceros

_____ **2.** Rosie the Riveter

_____ **3.** A. Phillip Randolph

_____ **4.** Norman Mineta

_____ **5.** zoot-suit riots

_____ **6.** Office of War Information

_____ **7.** Fair Employment Practices Committee

_____ **8.** internment

_____ **9.** Edward R. Murrow

_____ **10.** Carlos E. Castañeda

a. well-known radio correspondent famous for on-the-scene reports of the effects of the war on Europe

b. government agency that controlled the flow of war news in the United States

c. the symbol of patriotic female workers who labored in defense factories

d. African American labor leader who planned a protest march on Washington

e. created to enforce the presidential order forbidding racial discrimination in defense plants and government offices

f. Mexican farm and railroad workers who came to work in the U.S. Southwest during World War II

g. violent confrontations in Los Angeles between sailors and young Mexican American men

h. University of Texas history professor who fought to improve working conditions for Mexican Americans

i. the forced removal of people of Japanese descent to detention camps

j. Japanese American whose direct experience in an American detention camp fueled his later efforts to demand reparations for all Japanese Americans

■ POST-READING QUICK CHECK After you have finished reading the section, explain what made the following military units unique.

1. Blue Devils _____

2. The 442nd _____

CHAPTER
27

Americans in World War II

GUIDED READING STRATEGIES 27.3

■ **READING THE SECTION** As you read the section, list the key points for each heading.

1. Invasion of Italy

- _____
- _____
- _____

2. Battle of the Atlantic

- _____
- _____
- _____

3. D-Day

- _____
- _____
- _____

4. Dwight D. Eisenhower

- _____
- _____
- _____

5. George S. Patton

- _____
- _____
- _____

6. Holocaust

- _____
- _____
- _____

7. Vichy, France

- _____
- _____
- _____

8. Battle of the Bulge

- _____
- _____
- _____

9. Yalta Conference

- _____
- _____
- _____

■ **POST-READING QUICK CHECK** After you have finished reading the section, list three important things that allowed the Holocaust to be carried out.

1. _____

2. _____

3. _____

CHAPTER 27 Americans in World War II

GUIDED READING STRATEGIES 27.4

■ **READING THE SECTION** Each of the following sentences contains an under-lined word, phrase, or name that makes the sentence incorrect. As you read the sec-tion, use the space provided to write the word, phrase, or name that makes the sentence correct.

_____ 1. The United States pursued a policy of <u>island-skipping</u> as a way of attacking only strategic Japanese-held islands.

_____ 2. The last, largest, and most decisive naval battle of the Pacific was the <u>Battle of the Coral Sea</u>.

_____ 3. In the Battle of Leyte Gulf, the United States recaptured <u>New Guinea</u>.

_____ 4. At the Battle of Iwo Jima, <u>Japanese</u> troops were photographed raising their nation's flag in victory.

_____ 5. Japanese pilots who flew their planes into American ships, com-mitting suicide in the process, were called <u>hashimotos</u>.

_____ 6. The <u>Atom</u> Project was the top-secret attempt by the United States to construct an atom bomb.

_____ 7. The decision to drop the atomic bomb was made by President <u>Roosevelt</u>.

_____ 8. The first atomic bomb was dropped by the <u>Service Gray</u> on August 6, 1945.

_____ 9. The official surrender of the Japanese took place aboard the USS <u>Arizona</u>.

_____ 10. After the war, more than <u>1</u> percent of the homes in Düsseldorf, Germany, were uninhabitable.

■ **POST-READING QUICK CHECK** After you have finished reading the section, briefly explain some of the devastating effects of World War II.

_____

_____

_____

_____

The Cold War

CHAPTER 28

GUIDED READING STRATEGIES 28.1

■ **READING THE SECTION** As you read the section, match each of the following people with the correct description by writing the letter of the description in the space provided.

_____ **1.** Hideki Tōjō

_____ **2.** Adolf Eichmann

_____ **3.** Clement Atlee

_____ **4.** David Ben-Gurion

_____ **5.** Douglas MacArthur

_____ **6.** Folke Bernadotte

_____ **7.** Eleanor Roosevelt

_____ **8.** Trygve Lie

_____ **9.** Harry S Truman

_____ **10.** Ralph Bunche

a. American president at Potsdam Conference

b. Prime minister of Great Britain after Winston Churchill

c. American general who helped run Japan after World War II

d. Nazi official in charge of the Jewish extermination program during World War II

e. Premier of Japan during World War II

f. Norwegian who served as first secretary-general of the United Nations

g. U.S. representative to the United Nations who enjoyed a life of political and social activism

h. Zionist leader who had fought for a Jewish homeland since the early 1900s

i. Swedish count sent to the Middle East by the United Nations to mediate the Arab-Israeli War

j. U.S. diplomat sent to the Middle East by the United Nations to mediate the Arab-Israeli War

■ **POST-READING QUICK CHECK** After you have finished reading the section, state the two divisions of the United Nations and briefly describe their membership and purpose.

1. _____

_____

2. _____

_____

CHAPTER 28 The Cold War

GUIDED READING STRATEGIES 28.2

■■ READING THE SECTION As you read the section, use each clue below to write the term in the space provided. Then unscramble the boxed letters to identify the focus of Section 2.

1. Rivalry between the United States and the Soviet Union ___ ☐ ___ ___ ☐ ___ ___

2. Countries that are under Soviet control

___ ___ ☐ ___ ___ ___ ___ ___ ___   ___ ___ ___ ___ ☐ ___ ___

3. Restricting the expansion of communism ☐ ___ ___ ___ ___ ___ ___ ___ ___ ___ ___

4. Plan that created a special agency to inspect any nation's atomic-energy installations

___ ___ ___ ___ ☐ ___ ___ ___ ___

5. Act that set up the Atomic Energy Commission

___ ☐ ___ ___ ___ ___ ___   ___ ☐ ___ ___   ___ ___ ☐

6. Speech that President Truman gave emphasizing the need for foreign aid

___ ___ ___ ___ ___ ☐ ___ ___ ___ ___ ___ ___ ___

7. Economic aid to Europe ___ ___ ___ ☐ ___ ___ ___ ___ ___   ___ ☐ ___ ___

8. Transportation of food and supplies to West Berlin in 1948 and 1949

___ ☐ ___ ___ ___ ___   ___ ___ ___ ☐ ___ ___ ___ ___

9. United States-led military alliance ___ ☐ ___ ___

10. Soviet Union-led military alliance ☐ ___ ___ ___ ___ ___   ___ ___ ___ ___

Focus of Section 2: ☐☐☐ ☐☐☐☐ ☐☐☐ ☐☐☐☐☐☐☐

■■ POST-READING QUICK CHECK After you have finished reading the section, list three examples of how Stalin worked to maintain Soviet influence in Eastern Europe after the war.

1. _____

2. _____

3. _____

CHAPTER 28 The Cold War

GUIDED READING STRATEGIES 28.3

■ READING THE SECTION Review the list of events before reading the section. Then as you read the section, number the following events in the order in which they occurred.

_____ **1.** In the wake of the cease fire, President Truman pledges U.S. support of South Korea, and the UN Security Council urges other UN nations to pledge their support to South Korea as well.

_____ **2.** MacArthur calls for a major expansion of the war, and President Truman strongly disagrees.

_____ **3.** North Korea and South Korea set up separate governments, each claiming to rule the entire country of Korea.

_____ **4.** China joins the Korean War on the North Korean side.

_____ **5.** Dwight D. Eisenhower is elected president and fulfills his campaign promise to end the Korean War by using military force to get peace negotiations started.

_____ **6.** Outnumbered by the Chinese and North Korean troops, MacArthur's forces fall back and establish a stable defensive line near the 38th parallel.

_____ **7.** The United States helps to build up the South Korean army.

_____ **8.** The UN Security Council calls for an immediate cease-fire in Korea.

_____ **9.** The United States and the Soviet Union pull their troops out of Korea, leaving the two Korean armies to face each other at the 38th parallel.

_____ **10.** President Truman orders U.S. air and ground forces into action under the command of General Douglas MacArthur and the Korean War begins.

■ POST-READING QUICK CHECK After you have finished reading the section, in the space provided, discuss the U-2 incident and its significance.

_____

_____

_____

_____

_____

CHAPTER 28 · The Cold War

GUIDED READING STRATEGIES 28.4

■ **READING THE SECTION** As you read the section, complete the following outline by supplying the main idea and the missing subtopics and supporting details.

The Cold War at Home

Main Idea: _____

_____

Topic I: Fear stemming from the Cold War prompted the government to find ways to protect Americans from communism overseas.

   Detail A: _____

   Detail B: Soviet spies were identified and imprisoned or executed.

Topic II: Senator Joseph McCarthy led the search for Communists at home.

   Detail A: _____

   Detail B: _____

Topic III: _____

   Detail A: _____

   Detail B: Government launched a campaign to calm public fears about nuclear war.

   Detail C: _____

   Detail D: United States speeds up its space program to keep up with Soviets.

■ **POST-READING QUICK CHECK** After you have finished reading the section, in the space provided, list three ways that the United States streamlined its military to allow for peacetime rearmament.

1. _____

   _____

2. _____

   _____

3. _____

   _____

Society After World War II

CHAPTER 29

GUIDED READING STRATEGIES 29.1

■■ **READING THE SECTION** As you read the section, complete the following outline by supplying the main idea and the missing subtopics and supporting details.

The Challenges of Peace

Main Idea: _____

Topic I: _____.

    Detail A: _____

    Detail B: Congress passed the Employment Act of 1946 so the government would promote full employment and production.

    Detail C: _____

    Detail D: _____

    Detail E: _____

Topic II: The 1948 presidential election saw Harry S Truman, despite low public support, running for re-election.

    Detail A: _____

    Detail B: The Democratic Party split on the civil rights issue at the convention.

    Detail C: _____

    Detail D: Truman won the election in an upset.

Topic III: Truman asked Congress to pass a series of reforms called the Fair Deal.

    Detail A: _____

    Detail B: _____

■■ **POST-READING QUICK CHECK** After you have finished reading the section, list the three provisions of the Servicemen's Readjustment Act of 1944, more commonly known as the GI Bill of Rights.

  1. Provision: _____

  2. Provision: _____

  3. Provision: _____

Name _____ Class _____ Date _____

CHAPTER 29

Society After World War II

GUIDED READING STRATEGIES 29.2

■ READING THE SECTION As you read the section, complete the graphic organizer by supplying information about American life in the 1950s in each of the categories shown.

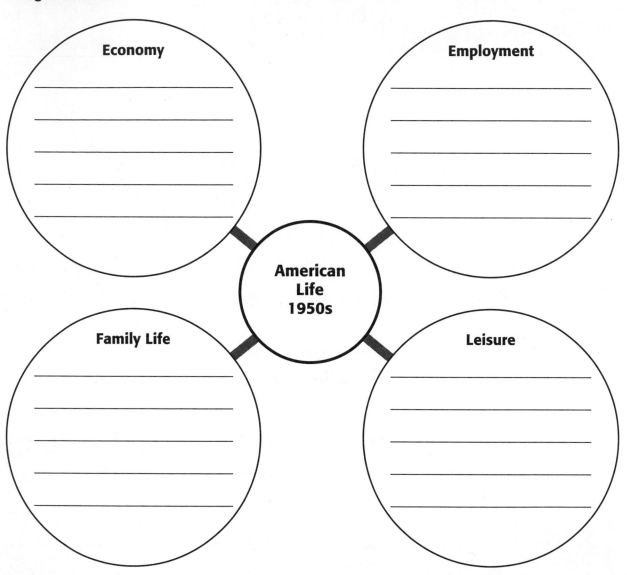

■ POST-READING QUICK CHECK After you have finished reading the section, in the space provided, explain the meaning of the term Modern Republicanism.

_____

_____

_____

CHAPTER
29

Society After World War II

GUIDED READING STRATEGIES 29.3

■ **READING THE SECTION** Review the list of events before reading the section. Then as you read the section, number the following events in the order in which they occurred.

_____ 1. As the bus boycott continues for months, white racists try every method from intimidation to physical violence to break it.

_____ 2. Rosa Parks is arrested for not giving up her bus seat to a white person.

_____ 3. Rosa Parks, an African American seamstress, attends a workshop on social justice that deeply influences her.

_____ 4. In Montgomery, 50,000 African Americans boycott the bus system.

_____ 5. Rosa Parks refuses to give up her bus seat to a white passenger.

_____ 6. King urges the African American community not to respond to violence with more violence, and the boycott continues.

_____ 7. NAACP leaders in Montgomery, Alabama, await a test case to challenge Montgomery's policy of forcing African Americans to ride in the back of city buses.

_____ 8. The Supreme Court rules both the Montgomery and the Alabama segregation laws unconstitutional.

_____ 9. By the end of 1956, Montgomery, Alabama, had a desegregated bus system.

_____ 10. A group of civil rights leaders from Montgomery, called the Montgomery Improvement Association, and their new spokesperson, Martin Luther King Jr., persuade the community to continue their bus boycott until the NAACP and Parks are done in the courts.

■ **POST-READING QUICK CHECK** After you have finished reading the section, in the space provided, discuss the two underlying societal problems that many writers and scholars felt were being ignored in the 1950s.

1. Problem: _____

_____

_____

2. Problem: _____

_____

_____

Name _____ Class _____ Date _____

CHAPTER 30 The New Frontier and the Great Society

GUIDED READING STRATEGIES 30.1

■ **READING THE SECTION** As you read the section, complete the following outline by supplying the main idea and the missing subtopics and supporting details.

Kennedy and the Cold War

Main Idea: President Kennedy's determination to fight communism led to several crises during his presidency.

Topic I: _____.

    Detail A: Richard Nixon was the Republican nominee.

    Detail B: _____
    Detail C: The televised debates helped Kennedy and hurt Nixon.

    Detail D: _____

Topic II: Kennedy's foreign policy was based on containing communism.

    Detail A: _____

    Detail B: _____
    Detail C: The Alliance for Progress offered aid to Latin American countries.

Topic III: _____

    Detail A: Kennedy hoped to trigger a popular uprising against Fidel Castro.

    Detail B: _____
    Detail C: The incident made America look weak.

Topic IV: The Berlin Crisis was another test for the Kennedy administration.
    Detail A: Soviet Union leader Nikita Khrushchev demanded that all Western troops must be removed from West Berlin.

    Detail B: _____

Topic V: The Cuban Missile Crisis brought the world to the brink of nuclear war.
    Detail A: Castro asked the Soviet Union to give him weapons for protection.

    Detail B: _____

    Detail C: _____

    Detail D: _____

■ **POST-READING QUICK CHECK** After you have finished reading the section, in the space provided, list two changes that came about as a result of the United States and the Soviet Union having such a close brush with nuclear war.

1. _____

2. _____

CHAPTER 30 The New Frontier and the Great Society

GUIDED READING STRATEGIES 30.2

■ **READING THE SECTION** As you read the section, examine each of the pairs of statements below. Circle the letter of the statement in each pair that is true.

1. **a.** John F. Kennedy was popular with many Americans because of his quick wit, good looks, and youthful demeanor.
   b. John F. Kennedy was popular with many Americans because he carried on the traditional ways of the Eisenhower presidency.

2. **a.** Many young Americans were turned off by politics during Kennedy's presidency.
   b. Many young Americans were motivated to go into politics and serve society during Kennedy's presidency.

3. **a.** Most of Kennedy's advisers were older men with much political experience but little education.
   b. Most of Kennedy's advisers were men with little political experience but a lot of education.

4. **a.** Kennedy's New Frontier program was intended to solve international problems.
   b. Kennedy's New Frontier program was intended to solve domestic problems.

5. **a.** Most of Kennedy's proposals were passed by Congress.
   b. Most of Kennedy's proposals were rejected by Congress.

6. **a.** Michael Harrington's book *The Other America* helped persuade Kennedy to create the Area Redevelopment Act.
   b. Michael Harrington's book *The Other America* persuaded Kennedy to veto the Area Redevelopment Act proposed by Congress.

7. **a.** Jack Ruby and Lee Harvey Oswald were arrested for the assassination of President Kennedy in Dallas, Texas.
   b. Dallas police arrested Lee Harvey Oswald for the shooting of Kennedy, but Oswald was shot two days later by Jack Ruby.

8. **a.** Chief Justice Earl Warren headed the Warren Commission, which ruled that Lee Harvey Oswald had acted alone in the assassination of Kennedy.
   b. The Warren Commission, investigating the assassination of Kennedy, ruled that there was most likely a conspiracy to kill the president.

■ **POST-READING QUICK CHECK** After you have finished reading the section, explain why Kennedy had conflicts with Congress.

_____

_____

_____

CHAPTER 30

The New Frontier and the Great Society

GUIDED READING STRATEGIES 30.3

■ **READING THE SECTION** As you read the section, complete the chart by placing the names of all of the programs and legislation put through by President Johnson in the appropriate columns.

Johnson's Great Society Programs and Legislation

Poverty	Health Care	Education
1. _____	1. _____	1. _____
2. _____	2. _____	
3. _____		
4. _____		

Housing	Culture	Environment
1. _____	1. _____	1. _____
2. _____	2. _____	2. _____
	3. _____	3. _____

■ **POST-READING QUICK CHECK** After you have finished reading the section, in the space provided, compare President Johnson's ability to get legislation passed in Congress with that of President Kennedy.

_____

_____

_____

_____

_____

_____

_____

_____

Guided Reading Strategies

The Civil Rights Movement

CHAPTER
31

GUIDED READING STRATEGIES 31.1

■ **READING THE SECTION** As you read the section, match each of the following people with the correct description by writing the letter of the description in the space provided.

_____ **1.** James Meredith

_____ **2.** Diane Nash

_____ **3.** Ross Barnett

_____ **4.** Medgar Evers

_____ **5.** Martin Luther King Jr.

_____ **6.** T. Eugene Connor

_____ **7.** Myrlie Evers

_____ **8.** Mohandas K. Gandhi

_____ **9.** Laurie Pritchett

_____ **10.** John Lewis

a. Southern Christian Leadership Conference leader who worked with the Freedom Riders

b. African American student whose registration at the University of Mississippi in 1962 caused a riot

c. Governor of Mississippi who strongly opposed school integration

d. Civil rights activist and wife of the NAACP field secretary

e. Field secretary for the NAACP who was assassinated in 1963

f. Police chief of Albany, Georgia, who arrested and jailed all of the nonviolent protesters in his city

g. Ordered police to attack civil rights marchers with dogs, fire hoses, and nightsticks

h. Leader of the independence movement in India whose nonviolent techniques influenced Martin Luther King Jr.

i. Freedom Rider who made a speech during the March on Washington

j. Leader of the Southern Christian Leadership Conference who gave a famous speech during the March on Washington

■ **POST-READING QUICK CHECK** After you have finished reading the section, in the space provided, state the names of three organizations dedicated to ending racial discrimination as described in Section 1 and also describe the makeup of their membership.

1. _____

2. _____

3. _____

The Civil Rights Movement

GUIDED READING STRATEGIES 31.2

■ **READING THE SECTION** Review the list of events before reading the section. Then as you read the section, number the following events in the correct order.

_____ **1.** Federal examiners descend upon the South to enforce the Voting Rights Act and register new African American voters.

_____ **2.** Marchers set out against Governor Wallace's wishes and are violently attacked by the police.

_____ **3.** For days African Americans who attempted to register to vote were beaten and arrested.

_____ **4.** Civil rights workers launch a registration drive in Selma, Alabama.

_____ **5.** Protesters begin their march again under the protection of federal marshals and the National Guard.

_____ **6.** Congress passes the Voting Rights Act of 1965.

_____ **7.** Civil rights leaders respond by calling a protest march from Selma to Montgomery on March 7.

_____ **8.** President Johnson asks for the speedy passage of a voting rights bill.

_____ **9.** Thousands of Americans pour into Montgomery to show support for the marchers.

_____ **10.** Alabama governor George Wallace bans the protest march.

■ **POST-READING QUICK CHECK** After you have finished reading the section, in the space provided, discuss what happened at the 1964 Democratic Convention to lead many activists to conclude that President Johnson and the Democratic Party could no longer be relied upon to advance their interests.

_____

_____

_____

_____

_____

_____

The Civil Rights Movement

CHAPTER 31

GUIDED READING STRATEGIES 31.3

■ **READING THE SECTION** As you read the section, complete the following chart by supplying the missing information about each of the civil rights organizations discussed in Section 3.

Civil Rights Organizations

Organization	Leader(s)	Main Belief/Use of Violence
Southern Christian Leadership Conference (SCLC)	_____	Integration _____
_____	Elijah Muhammed	_____ Violence used
Black Power	_____	Black separatism _____
_____	_____ _____	Black political group Violence used

■ **POST-READING QUICK CHECK** After you have finished reading the section, in the space provided, give three reasons why the civil rights movement began to break apart.

1. _____

_____

2. _____

_____

3. _____

_____

CHAPTER 31 — The Civil Rights Movement

GUIDED READING STRATEGIES 31.4

■ **READING THE SECTION** As you read the section, complete the graphic organizers by supplying the missing information about each of these important court cases from the 1970s. The graphic organizers are arranged in chronological order.

Important Civil Rights Court Cases of the 1970s

Court case: *Griggs* v. *Duke Power Co.* Year occurred: _____

Outcome: _____

_____

_____

Court case: _____ Year occurred: 1974

Outcome: _____

_____

_____

Court case: _____ Year occurred: _____

Outcome: The Supreme Court ruled that a white man, Allan Bakke, had been unfairly denied admission to medical school on the basis of quotas. The Court did not rule out all forms of affirmative action, but it did strike down the quota system.

■ **POST-READING QUICK CHECK** After you have finished reading the section, in the space provided, write a brief summary of the status of each of the following civil rights organizations at the beginning of the 1970s.

1. SCLC: _____

2. SNCC: _____

3. Black Panthers: _____

4. Black Muslims: _____

CHAPTER 32

Struggles for Change

GUIDED READING STRATEGIES 32.1

■■ **READING THE SECTION** As you read the section, complete the following chart by listing six examples of progress in the women's movement and two examples of opposition to the women's movement as stated in Section 1.

The Women's Movement

Progress	Opposition
1. _____ _____	1. _____ _____
2. _____ _____	2. _____ _____
3. _____ _____	
4. _____ _____	
5. _____ _____	
6. _____ _____	

■■ **POST-READING QUICK CHECK** After you have finished reading the section, in the space provided, list three ways that President Kennedy responded to the problems faced by working women.

1. _____

_____

2. _____

3. _____

CHAPTER 32

Struggles for Change

GUIDED READING STRATEGIES 32.2

■ **READING THE SECTION** As you read the section, match each of the descriptions with the name of the person being described by writing the correct letter in the space provided.

_____ **1.** A labor union organizer who founded the National Farm Workers Association (NFWA) was
  a. César Chávez.
  b. Rodolfo Gonzales.
  c. José Angel Gutiérrez.
  d. Henry B. Gonzalez.

_____ **2.** A former CSO worker who assisted with the organization of the NFWA was
  a. José Angel Gutiérrez.
  b. Reies López Tijerina.
  c. Delores Huerta.
  d. David Cargo.

_____ **3.** A Catholic priest who influenced César Chávez was
  a. Carlos Munoz.
  b. Rodolfo Gonzales.
  c. Henry B. Gonzalez.
  d. Donald McDonnell.

_____ **4.** He organized an NFWA strike against grape growers.
  a. Carlos Munoz
  b. César Chávez
  c. Reies López Tijerina
  d. David Cargo

_____ **5.** An organizer of the Alianza Federal de Mercedes was
  a. Reies López Tijerina.
  b. José Angel Gutiérrez.
  c. Donald McDonnell.
  d. Henry B. Gonzalez.

_____ **6.** A leader of the *aliancistas* was
  a. José Angel Gutiérrez.
  b. Reies López Tijerina.
  c. Rodolfo Gonzales.
  d. César Chávez.

_____ **7.** The founder of the Crusade for Justice was
  a. Reies López Tijerina.
  b. Rodolfo Gonzales.
  c. José Angel Gutiérrez.
  d. Gil Padilla.

_____ **8.** A leader of the Mexican American Youth Organization (MAYO) was
  a. César Chávez.
  b. Donald McDonnell.
  c. Carlos Munoz.
  d. José Angel Gutiérrez.

■ **POST-READING QUICK CHECK** After you have finished reading the section, in the space provided, list three different positive results of the Chicano movement.

1. _____

2. _____

3. _____

Guided Reading Strategies

CHAPTER 32 Struggles for Change

GUIDED READING STRATEGIES 32.3

■■ **READING THE SECTION** As you read the section, complete the following outline by supplying the main idea and the missing subtopics and supporting details.

More Groups Mobilize

Main Idea: _____

Topic I: American Indians began organizing in the 1960s.
   Detail A: Red Power activists occupied the old Alcatraz prison.

   Detail B: _____
   Detail C: "Trail of Broken Treaties" protesters occupied Bureau of Indian Affairs offices in Washington, D.C.

   Detail D: _____
   Detail E: Other American Indians worked out their problems in the courts and through political lobbying.

Topic II: People with disabilities, such as Ed Roberts, fought for their rights.

   Detail A: _____
   Detail B: Congress passed the Education for All Handicapped Children Act in 1975.

Topic III: _____

   Detail A: _____
   Detail B: National Council of Senior Citizens (NCSC) represented the needs of lower-income older Americans.

   Detail C: _____
   Detail D: Congress passed the Older Americans Act in 1965.

Topic IV: _____
   Detail A: The *In Re Gault* Supreme Court case of 1967 concerned children's rights.

   Detail B: _____

   Detail C: _____

■■ **POST-READING QUICK CHECK** After you have finished reading the section, in the space provided, state the four key points of the Children's Bill of Rights.

1. _____

2. _____

3. _____

4. _____

Struggles for Change

CHAPTER 32

GUIDED READING STRATEGIES 32.4

■ **READING THE SECTION** Each of the following sentences contains an underlined word, name, or phrase that makes the sentence incorrect. As you read the section, use the space provided to write the word, phrase, or name that makes the sentence correct.

_____ 1. The rift between the baby boomers and their parents in the 1960s came to be called the <u>understanding gap</u>.

_____ 2. Young Americans in the 1960s who were seeking an alternative way of life were called <u>dropouts</u>.

_____ 3. The <u>commune culture</u> was the large group of American young people who rejected the values and customs of American society.

_____ 4. Many young Americans set up <u>hippie-villes</u> to live in a shared, collective way in line with their values.

_____ 5. <u>SDL</u> was a mind-altering drug popularized in the 1960s by Timothy Leary.

_____ 6. An art style popular in the 1960s, <u>regular art</u>, was created to show people that simple, everyday objects could be viewed as art.

_____ 7. <u>Heavy metal</u> was a musical style that gained in popularity during the 1960s.

_____ 8. <u>Hop</u> music regained its popularity in the 1960s as more young people began to listen to artists such as Joan Baez.

_____ 9. African American music made popular by the Motown Records company in the 1960s was called <u>beat</u>.

_____ 10. The huge music and art festival held in upstate New York in 1969 was called <u>Rockstock</u>.

■ **POST-READING QUICK CHECK** After you have finished reading the section, in the space provided, list three reasons that led many young Americans to question the values of American society in the 1960s.

1. _____

2. _____

3. _____

Guided Reading Strategies

War in Vietnam

GUIDED READING STRATEGIES 33.1

■ **READING THE SECTION** As you read the section, match each of the following people or terms with the correct description by writing the letter of the description in the space provided.

_____ **1.** French Indochina

_____ **2.** Vietminh

_____ **3.** Mekong Delta

_____ **4.** Vietcong

_____ **5.** domino theory

_____ **6.** Le Loi

_____ **7.** John F. Kennedy

_____ **8.** communism

_____ **9.** Ho Chi Minh

_____ **10.** Ngo Dinh Diem

a. Center of Vietnam's population in the south

b. Vietnamese guerrilla fighter who used the support of the people to help drive out the Chinese in the 1400s

c. Country created by combining Vietnam, Laos, and Cambodia

d. Vietnamese nationalist whose chosen name means "He Who Enlightens"

e. Another name for the League for the Independence of Vietnam

f. Philosophy of the Vietnamese nationalists whom Truman would not support

g. A term for Eisenhower's belief that if Vietnam fell to the Communists, all the other countries in Southeast Asia would follow

h. Unpopular first president of the Republic of Vietnam

i. Rebel members of the National Liberation Front whose main goal was the overthrow of Ngo Dinh Diem's government

j. Person whose desire to bolster world opinion of the United States after the Bay of Pigs issue caused him to lead the United States further into the Vietnamese conflict

■ **POST-READING QUICK CHECK** After you have finished reading the section, briefly explain Ho Chi Minh's method of warfare against the French.

_____

_____

_____

_____

_____

War in Vietnam

GUIDED READING STRATEGIES 33.2

■ **READING THE SECTION** As you read the section, examine the riddles below. Solve each riddle by writing the correct name or term in the space provided.

_____ 1. "I am the U.S. secretary of defense who advised President Johnson to increase the U.S. military involvement in Vietnam."

_____ 2. "I am the act of Congress that gave President Johnson the right to use military force as he saw fit against the North Vietnamese."

_____ 3. "I am the large-scale bombing campaign against military targets in North Vietnam."

_____ 4. "My twisting network of jungle paths throughout North Vietnam allowed the North Vietnamese to bring weapons and supplies to South Vietnam."

_____ 5. "I can destroy thousands of acres of vegetation at one time."

_____ 6. "I am a military strategy of moving residents to refugee camps or cities, and then burning the villages where they lived, to prevent the North Vietnamese from gaining territory."

_____ 7. "I'm a radical antiwar group that held many protests."

_____ 8. "While head of the Foreign Relations Committee, I was strongly opposed to U.S. involvement in the war in Vietnam."

■ **POST-READING QUICK CHECK** After you have finished reading the section, briefly explain how the media affected people's opinions about American involvement in the Vietnam War.

_____

_____

_____

_____

_____

_____

War in Vietnam

GUIDED READING STRATEGIES 33.3

■ **READING THE SECTION** As you read the section, list three key points under each topic indicated in the graphic organizer.

1. Tet Offensive	4. Henry Kissinger	7. Antiwar Protests
• _____	• _____	• _____
• _____	• _____	• _____
• _____	• _____	• _____
2. The Election of 1968	5. Vietnamization	8. Pentagon Papers
• _____	• _____	• _____
• _____	• _____	• _____
• _____	• _____	• _____
3. Democratic National Convention	6. Invasion of Cambodia	9. Madman Theory
• _____	• _____	• _____
• _____	• _____	• _____
• _____	• _____	• _____

■ **POST-READING QUICK CHECK** After you have finished reading the section, briefly explain who Nixon was referring to with the term "silent majority."

_____

_____

_____

_____

War in Vietnam

GUIDED READING STRATEGIES 33.4

■ **READING THE SECTION** As you read the section, circle the boldface word or phrase that best completes each statement below.

1. The official voting age was changed to **18/21** to increase the number of women, minorities, and young people in political party organizations.

2. Strongly opposed to the war, **George McGovern/Robert Kennedy** won the 1972 Democratic presidential nomination.

3. American citizens were part of a massive evacuation from **Da Nang/Saigon** when the North Vietnamese invaded South Vietnam.

4. **Le Ly Hayslip/Maya Ying Lin** was a Vietnamese immigrant who founded a charitable organization to provide comfort to victims of war.

5. **Agent Orange/DDT** was found to cause many types of cancer and birth defects after its use in the Vietnam War.

6. The **War Powers Act/Twenty-sixth Amendment** placed a 60-day limit on a president's putting American troops into battle in foreign conflicts.

7. The Vietnam War showed that public opinion **could/could not** influence a government's decision to use military force in foreign countries.

8. **Le Ly Hayslip/Maya Ying Lin** designed the Vietnam War Memorial.

■ **POST-READING QUICK CHECK** After you have finished reading the section, list two long-term effects the Vietnam War had on the Vietnamese people and two long-term effects on the United States.

Vietnamese people:

1. _____

2. _____

United States:

1. _____

2. _____

Name _____ Class _____ Date _____

From Nixon to Carter

GUIDED READING STRATEGIES 34.1

■ **READING THE SECTION** As you read the section, complete the following outline by supplying the main idea and the missing subtopics and supporting details.

The Nixon Years

Main Idea: Richard Nixon's presidential style was different from his Democratic predecessors.

Topic I: Nixon attempted to reform the welfare system.

    Detail A: _____

Topic II: _____

    There was stagflation in America when Nixon took over.

Topic III: The energy crisis occurred in 1973.

    Detail A: _____

    Detail B: _____

    Detail C: _____

Topic IV: _____

    Detail A: The Environmental Protection Agency (EPA) was formed.

    Detail B: _____

Topic V: Nixon's main interest was foreign affairs.

    Detail A: _____

    Detail B: _____

    Detail C: _____

    Detail D: The Strategic Arms Limitation Talks limited the number of intercontinental nuclear missiles.

    Detail E: _____

■ **POST-READING QUICK CHECK** After you have finished reading the section, in the space provided, describe two different world "trouble spots" to which Nixon had to respond.

1. _____

2. _____

CHAPTER 34

From Nixon to Carter

GUIDED READING STRATEGIES 34.2

■ **READING THE SECTION** As you read the section, complete the following outline by supplying the main idea and the missing subtopics and supporting details.

From Watergate to Ford

Main Idea: _____

Topic I: Nixon began to hide information from Congress and behave as though there should be no limitations on his power.

    Detail A: _____

    Detail B: _____
    Detail C: The men who staged the break-in were paid by Nixon's campaign organization, Committee to Re-elect the President.
    Detail D: Congress began to officially investigate the scandal known as Watergate.

Topic II: _____

    Detail A: _____
    Detail B: The Saturday Night Massacre occurred when the Special Prosecutor investigating Nixon was fired.

    Detail C: _____
    Detail D: On August 8, 1974, Nixon resigned the presidency.

Topic III: After Nixon, Gerald Ford became president.

    Detail A: Ford granted Nixon a full pardon, allowing him to go unpunished.

    Detail B: _____
    Detail C: Because Congress was controlled by Democrats and Ford was a Republican, he vetoed 66 bills.

    Detail D: _____

Topic IV: _____
    Detail A: Ford's involvement in the *Mayaguez* incident won him points with the American public.

    Detail B: _____

■ **POST-READING QUICK CHECK** After you have finished reading the section, in the space provided, explain why Ford's handling of Nixon and the Vietnam War draft evaders affected his approval rating.

_____

_____

CHAPTER 34 **From Nixon to Carter**

GUIDED READING STRATEGIES 34.3

■ **READING THE SECTION** As you read the section, match each of the following people or terms with the correct description by writing the letter of the description in the space provided.

_____ 1. Three Mile Island

_____ 2. National Energy Act

_____ 3. Camp David Accords

_____ 4. Anwar Sadat

_____ 5. apartheid

_____ 6. Department of Energy

_____ 7. Jimmy Carter

_____ 8. Menachem Begin

_____ 9. 1980 Summer Olymics

_____ 10. Panama Canal Treaties

a. Candidate whose presidential campaign emphasized a new approach to government that would ensure ethical and honest activity

b. Legislation proposed by Carter, ultimately greatly adjusted by the Senate, to help the energy crisis

c. Government group whose function is to oversee American energy issues

d. Nuclear plant whose failed reactor resulted in shaken public confidence in nuclear energy as a source of power

e. Agreement that Panama would gain control of the Panama Canal operations by the year 2000

f. South African social policy of rule by the white minority, while denying rights to the black majority

g. Carter boycotted this after the Soviet Union's invasion of Afghanistan

h. Agreements reached during Carter's meetings with Menachem Begin and Anwar Sadat to achieve peace in the Middle East

i. Israeli prime minister who signed a formal peace treaty with Egypt that ended 30 years of warfare in the Middle East

j. Egyptian president who shared the 1978 Nobel Peace Prize with the Israeli prime minister for their efforts toward securing peace in the Middle East

■ **POST-READING QUICK CHECK** After you have finished reading the section, answer the following questions on this section's content.

1. What actions did President Carter take to stimulate the economy?

_____

2. Why did the Carter family walk to the White House on Inauguration Day?

_____

From Nixon to Carter

GUIDED READING STRATEGIES 34.4

READING THE SECTION As you read the section, examine each of the pairs of statements below. Circle the letter of the statement in each pair that is true.

1. a. The Voting Rights Act of 1975 required that voting materials be in a variety of foreign languages for those who did not speak English.
 b. The Bilingual Education Act required that voting materials be in a variety of foreign languages for those who did not speak English.

2. a. The Foreign Language Act encouraged public schools to teach non-English-speaking students in their traditional language.
 b. The Bilingual Education Act encouraged public schools to teach non-English-speaking students in their traditional language.

3. a. Many Americans flocked to the Sunbelt, the southwestern area of the United States, because of economic growth and a better climate.
 b. Few Americans flocked to the Sunbelt, the southwestern area of the United States, because of economic stagnation and a harsh climate.

4. a. Author Tom Wolfe described the 1970s as the I Decade because people were selfish and self-absorbed.
 b. Author Tom Wolfe described the 1970s as the Me Decade because people were selfish and self-absorbed.

5. a. The 1970s saw the decline of the self-help movement, in which Americans worked to improve their physical, emotional, and intellectual selves.
 b. The 1970s saw the rise of the self-help movement, in which Americans worked to improve their physical, emotional, and intellectual selves.

6. a. Neil Armstrong and Edwin Aldrin were the first astronauts to land on the Moon as a result of their *Apollo 13* space flight.
 b. Neil Armstrong and Edwin Aldrin were the first astronauts to land on the Moon as a result of their *Apollo 11* space flight.

7. a. *Skylab* was an unsuccessful space station placed in orbit by the Soviet Union in 1973.
 b. *Skylab* was a successful space station placed in orbit by the United States in 1973.

8. a. Steven Jobs and Stephen Wozniak built the first personal computer in a garage.
 b. Steven Jobs and Stephen Wozniak built the first personal computer at Stanford University.

POST-READING QUICK CHECK After you have finished reading the section, briefly explain the significance of the following people to lifestyle changes in the 1970s.

Werner Erhard   Significance: _____

Maharishi Mahesh Yogi Significance: _____

The Republican Revolution

GUIDED READING STRATEGIES 35.1

■ **READING THE SECTION** As you read the section, list three key points under each topic indicated in the graphic organizer.

1. **Iran Hostage Crisis**

   • _____

   • _____

   • _____

2. **The New Right**

   • _____

   • _____

   • _____

3. **Reaganomics**

   • _____

   • _____

   • _____

4. **Critics' Views of Reaganomics**

   • _____

   • _____

   • _____

5. **Strategic Defense Initiative (SDI)**

   • _____

   • _____

   • _____

6. **Solidarity**

   • _____

   • _____

   • _____

7. **Lech Walesa**

   • _____

   • _____

   • _____

8. **Sandinistas**

   • _____

   • _____

   • _____

9. **El Salvador**

   • _____

   • _____

   • _____

■ **POST-READING QUICK CHECK** After you have finished reading the section, briefly explain the significance of the following people to President Reagan's administration.

Ayatollah Khomeini   Significance: _____

_____

Jerry Falwell   Significance: _____

_____

The Republican Revolution

GUIDED READING STRATEGIES 35.2

■ **READING THE SECTION** As you read the section, examine the riddles below. Solve each riddle by writing the correct name or term in the space provided.

_____ 1. "I was a unique candidate for vice president."

_____ 2. "No one like me has ever sat on the Supreme Court before."

_____ 3. "As long as I'm around, the budget will be balanced via forced spending cuts."

_____ 4. "I am the illegal practice of using confidential stock market information for personal gain."

_____ 5. "I began when many banks and savings and loans went bankrupt."

_____ 6. "I am the scandal in which money was illegally sent to the United States–supported Nicaraguan rebels."

_____ 7. "I made enormous changes in the Soviet Union."

_____ 8. "Anyone who likes freedom will like what I have to offer, especially in the Soviet Union."

_____ 9. "I refer to a Russian leader's plan to restructure the Soviet economy and government."

_____ 10. "Flying weapons of mass destruction would no longer be in Europe after I was signed."

■ **POST-READING QUICK CHECK** After you have finished reading the section, briefly explain the legal consequences Oliver North faced for his involvement in the Iran-Contra affair.

_____

_____

_____

_____

_____

CHAPTER 35 The Republican Revolution

GUIDED READING STRATEGIES 35.3

■ **READING THE SECTION** As you read the section, fill in the missing information in the graphic organizer.

1. **Person:** _____

   Key Point: First civilian to be part of a space shuttle crew. One of seven crew members killed when *Challenger* exploded shortly after takeoff.

2. **Term:** acquired immune deficiency syndrome (AIDS)

   Key Point: _____

   _____

   _____

   _____

3. **Person:** _____

   Key Point: Prominent African American who sought the 1988 Democratic presidential nomination. Hoped to attract a "Rainbow Coalition" of supporters.

4. **Term:** _____

   Key Point: After breaking away from the Soviet Union, Belarus, Russia, and Ukraine formed a loose confederation that several more former Soviet states eventually joined.

5. **Term:** Operation Desert Storm

   Key Point: _____

   _____

   _____

   _____

6. **Person:** _____

   Key Point: African American general who was chairman of the Joint Chiefs of Staff during Operation Desert Storm.

7. **Term:** War on Drugs

   Key Point: _____

   _____

   _____

   _____

8. **Person:** _____

   Key Point: Her accusations of sexual harassment against Supreme Court nominee Clarence Thomas stirred nationwide debate.

■ **POST-READING QUICK CHECK** After you have finished reading the section, briefly explain the purpose of the Americans with Disabilities Act. Then list at least two benefits it provides people with physical or mental disabilities.

_____

_____

_____

CHAPTER 36 Launching the New Millennium

GUIDED READING STRATEGIES 36.1

■ **READING THE SECTION** Each of the following sentences contains an underlined word, name, or phrase that makes the sentence incorrect. As you read the section, use the space provided to write the word, phrase, or name that makes the sentence correct.

_____ 1. Clarence Thomas captured 19 percent of the vote in the 1992 presidential election because of his "third-party" appeal.

_____ 2. 1992 was the year of the young in American politics.

_____ 3. Operation Restore Hope was a Republican program that promised a balanced budget amendment and other reforms.

_____ 4. When Republicans took control of both the Senate and the House, Ross Perot was elected Speaker.

_____ 5. In the first election in South Africa in which all races of people could vote, Mu'ammar Gadhafi was elected president.

_____ 6. The Contract with America was launched to end the famine in Somalia.

_____ 7. Palestinian leader Yasir Arafat met with Israeli leader Menachem Begin to negotiate a peace between Jews and Arabs.

_____ 8. The Libyan leader tied to several terrorist incidents is Nelson Mandela.

■ **POST-READING QUICK CHECK** After you have finished reading the section, briefly explain Bill Clinton's statement during his 1992 campaign that voters would be getting "two for the price of one" if he were elected.

_____

_____

_____

_____

_____

_____

Launching the New Millennium

CHAPTER 36

GUIDED READING STRATEGIES 36.2

■ **READING THE SECTION** As you read the section, fill in the missing information in the graphic organizer.

1. **Person:** _____

   Key Point: Republican challenger to Clinton's re-election was a World War II veteran who suffered from an inability to be an effective speaker.

2. **Term:** economic boom

   Key Point: _____

   _____

   _____

   _____

   _____

3. **Term:** _____

   Key Point: Violent racial confrontations spurred by the acquittal of four Los Angeles police officers who had been accused of beating an African American motorist.

4. **Term:** _____

   Key Point: An effort launched by President Clinton to try to discuss racial issues and concerns.

5. **Person:** Kenneth Starr

   Key Point: _____

   _____

   _____

   _____

6. **Term:** _____

   Key Point: For only the second time in U.S. history, the House of Representatives voted on December 20, 1998, to take this action.

7. **Person:** Slobodan Milosevic

   Key Point: _____

   _____

   _____

   _____

8. **Person:** _____

   Key Point: Born in Czechoslovakia, became U.S. secretary of state and played a very important role in the Kosovo crisis.

■ **POST-READING QUICK CHECK** After you have finished reading the section, briefly explain the basis for the criticism that Kenneth Starr's investigation received.

_____

_____

_____

CHAPTER 36 Launching the New Millennium

GUIDED READING STRATEGIES 36.3

■ **READING THE SECTION** As you read the section, fill in the missing information in the graphic organizer.

Technology and Society

Space Developments	Computer Developments	Concerns
• _____	• _____	• _____
• _____	• _____	• _____
• _____	• _____	• _____
• _____	• _____	• _____

■ **POST-READING QUICK CHECK** After you have finished reading the section, briefly explain the significance of the following people:

Bill Gates   Significance: _____

Shannon Lucid   Significance: _____

Launching the New Millennium

GUIDED READING STRATEGIES 36.4

■ **READING THE SECTION** As you read the section, match each of the following terms or people with the correct description by writing the letter of the description in the space provided.

_____ **1.** multinational corporations

_____ **2.** Al Gore

_____ **3.** economic

_____ **4.** Chernobyl disaster

_____ **5.** George W. Bush

_____ **6.** European Union (EU)

_____ **7.** recycling

_____ **8.** North American Free Trade Agreement

_____ **9.** biomass

_____ **10.** International Telephone and Telegraph (IT&T)

a. The only type of big questions that will confront the world in the future, according to Bruce W. Nelan

b. Western European trading bloc designed to allow for the free movement of goods, labor, and capital among member nations

c. Provides for a lowering of trade barriers among the United States, Mexico, and Canada

d. Companies that invest money in a variety of business ventures around the world

e. American company that has expanded its investments in many countries outside the United States

f. Nuclear accident in Ukraine that put 50 times more radioactive material in the air than the two bombs dropped on Hiroshima and Nagasaki combined

g. Materials such as wood or waste products that can be burned or used to make fuel

h. Democratic candidate for president in 2000

i. Term for the collection and processing of waste items for reuse

j. Republican candidate for president in 2000

■ **POST-READING QUICK CHECK** After you have finished reading the section, briefly discuss the issues that you think will be at the center of U.S. concern during the first decade of the 2000s.

_____

_____

_____

_____

_____